- Paperback Edition -

TRIUMPH
TR6

Other Veloce publications -

• **Colour Family Album Series** •
Alfa Romeo by Andrea & David Sparrow
Bubblecars & Microcars by Andrea & David Sparrow
Bubblecars & Microcars, More by Andrea & David Sparrow
Citroën 2CV by Andrea & David Sparrow
Citroën DS by Andrea & David Sparrow
Fiat & Abarth 500 & 600 by Andrea & David Sparrow
Lambretta by Andrea & David Sparrow
Mini & Mini Cooper by Andrea & David Sparrow
Motor Scooters by Andrea & David Sparrow
Porsche by Andrea & David Sparrow
Triumph Sportscars by Andrea & David Sparrow
Vespa by Andrea & David Sparrow
VW Beetle by Andrea & David Sparrow
VW Beetle/Bug, Custom by Andrea & David Sparrow
VW Bus, Camper, Van & Pick-up by Andrea & David Sparrow

• **SpeedPro Series** •
How to Blueprint & Build a 4-Cylinder Engine Short Block for High Performance by Des Hammill
How to Build a V8 Engine Short Block for High Performance by Des Hammill
How to Build & Modify Sportscar/Kitcar Suspension & Brakes for High Performance by Des Hammill
How to Build & Power Tune SU Carburettors by Des Hammill
How to Build & Power Tune Weber DCOE & Dellorto DHLA Carburetors by Des Hammill
How to Build & Power Tune Harley-Davidson Evolution Engines by Des Hammill
How to Build & Power Tune Distributor-type Ignition Systems by Des Hammill
How to Build, Modify & Power Tune Cylinder Heads by Peter Burgess
How to Choose & Time Camshafts for Maximum Power by Des Hammill
How to Give your MGB V8 Power Updated & Revised Edition by Roger Williams
How to Improve MGB, MGC, MGB V8 by Roger Williams
How to Modify Volkswagen Beetle Chassis, Suspension & Brakes for High Performance by James Hale
How to Plan & Build a Fast Road Car by Daniel Stapleton
How to Power Tune BMC/BL/Rover 1275cc A Series Engines by Des Hammill
How to Power Tune BMC/BL/Rover 998cc A Series Engines by Des Hammill
How to Power Tune Jaguar XK Engines by Des Hammill
How to Power Tune the MGB 4-Cylinder Engine by Peter Burgess
How to Power Tune the MG Midget & Austin-Healey Sprite for Road & Track Updated, Revised & Enlarged Edition by Daniel Stapleton
How to Power Tune Alfa Romeo Twin Cam Engines by Jim Kartalamakis
How to Power Tune Ford SOHC 'Pinto' & Sierra Cosworth DOHC Engines by Des Hammill

• **General** •
Alfa Romeo Berlinas by John Tipler
Alfa Romeo Giulia Coupé GT & GTA by John Tipler
Automotive Mascots by David Kay & Lynda Springate
Bentley Continental, Corniche & Azure 1951-1998 by Martin Bennett
British Cars, The Complete Catalogue of 1895-1975 by Culshaw & Horrobin
British Trailer Caravans & their Manufacturers 1919-1959 by Andrew Jenkinson
British Trailer Caravans & their Manufacturers from 1960 by Andrew Jenkinson
Bugatti Type 40 by Barrie Price & Jean-Louis Arbey
Bugatti 46/50 Updated & Revised Edition by Barrie Price
Bugatti 57 - The Last French Bugatti 2nd Edition by Barrie Price
Chrysler 300 - America's Most Powerful Car by Robert Ackerson
Cobra - The Real Thing! by Trevor Legate
Cortina - Ford's Bestseller by Graham Robson
Daimler SP250 'Dart' by Brian Long
Datsun/Nissan 280ZX & 300ZX by Brian Long
Datsun Z - From Fairlady to 280Z by Brian Long
Dune Buggy Handbook by James Hale
Fiat & Abarth 124 Spider & Coupé by John Tipler
Fiat & Abarth 500 & 600 (revised edition) by Malcolm Bobbitt
Ford F100/F150 Pick-up by Robert Ackerson
Grey Guide by Dave Thornton
Jaguar XJS by Brian Long
Jim Redman - Six Times World Motorcycle Champion by Jim Redman
Lea-Francis Story by Barrie Price
Lexus Story by Brian Long
Lola - The Illustrated History (1957-1977) by John Starkey
Lola T70 - The Racing History & Individual Chassis Record New Edition by John Starkey
Lotus 49 by Michael Oliver
Mazda MX5/Miata 1.6 Enthusiast's Workshop Manual by Rod Grainger & Pete Shoemark
Mazda MX5/Miata 1.8 Enthusiast's Workshop Manual by Rod Grainger & Pete Shoemark
Mazda MX5 - Renaissance Sportscar by Brian Long
MGA - First of a New Line by John Price Williams
Motor Museums of the British Isles & Republic of Ireland by David Burke & Tom Price
Nuvolari: When Nuvolari Raced ... by Valerio Moretti
Porsche 356 by Brian Long
Porsche 911R, RS & RSR 4th Edition by John Starkey
Porsche 914 & 914-6 by Brian Long
Porsche 924 by Brian Long
Prince & I by Princess Ceril Birabongse
Rolls-Royce Silver Shadow/Bentley T Series, Corniche & Camargue Updated & Revised Edition by Malcolm Bobbitt
Rolls-Royce Silver Spirit, Silver Spur & Bentley Mulsanne by Malcolm Bobbitt
Rolls-Royce Silver Wraith, Dawn & Cloud/Bentley MkVI, R & S Series by Martyn Nutland
Singer Story: Cars, Commercial Vehicles, Bicycles & Motorcycles by Kevin Atkinson
Taxi! The Story of the 'London' Taxicab by Malcolm Bobbitt
Triumph TR6 by William Kimberley
Triumph Motorcycles & the Meriden Factory by Hughie Hancox
Triumph Tiger Cub Bible by Mike Estall
Turner's Triumphs - Edward Turner & his Triumph Motorcycles by Jeff Clew
Veloce Guide to the Top 100 Used Touring Caravans by Andrew Jenkinson
Velocette Motorcycles - MSS to Thruxton by Rod Burris
Volkswagens of the World by Simon Glen
VW Bus, Camper, Van, Pickup by Malcolm Bobbitt
Works Rally Mechanic by Brian Moylan

First published in 1995 by Veloce Publishing Plc., 33 Trinity Street, Dorchester DT1 1TT, England. Fax 01305 268864. This paperback edition published 1998. Reprinted 2000.

ISBN 1 901295-20-6/UPC 36847 00120-9

© William Kimberley and Veloce Publishing Plc 1995, 1998 & 2000.

All rights reserved. With the exception of quoting brief passages for the purpose of review, no part of this publication may be recorded, reproduced or transmitted/any means, including photocopying, without the written permission of Veloce Publishing Plc.
Throughout this book logos, model names and designations, etc, have been used for the purposes of identification, illustration and decoration. Such names are the property of the trademark holder as this is not an official publication.
Readers with ideas for automotive books, or books on other transport or related hobby subjects, are invited to write to the editorial director of Veloce Publishing at the above address.
British Library Cataloguing in Publication Data -
A catalogue record for this book is available from the British Library.
Typesetting (Bookman), design and page make-up all/Veloce on Apple Mac.
Printed in Spain.

Visit Veloce on the Web - www.veloce.co.uk

- Paperback Edition -

TRIUMPH
TR6

William Kimberley

VELOCE PUBLISHING PLC
PUBLISHERS OF FINE AUTOMOTIVE BOOKS

ACKNOWLEDGEMENTS

There are many people who helped me in writing this book; some are experts on the TR6, others, pure enthusiasts who love the car for what it is. My first vote of thanks, though, must go to the guru who is both expert and enthusiast and much more besides. To many he is the godfather not just of Triumph TRs but of the postwar British sports car. The man in question is Harry Webster who kindly let me take his time to ply him with questions which he graciously answered.

Experts who have been willing to pass on their knowledge to me have included Dave Lewis, doyen of the TR Register and Steve Divall, editor of *The TR Driver*. Each has been a mine of information, Dave Lewis, in particular, showing me - in minute detail - just what it takes to turn a dustbin-load of tired and rusty parts into a show car. The patience and attention to detail required just cannot be overstated.

Peter Cox of Cox & Buckles, now part of Moss Europe Ltd., was very informative about the Heritage shells and the problems therein, while his enthusiasm for the Cox & Buckles TR Championship was highly infectious. Daryl Uprichard of Racetorations was just as illuminating on what it takes to turn an ordinary TR6 into something very special. He was also extremely helpful in pointing out what to avoid when buying secondhand.

Photographs have been acquired from many sources but those who deserve special thanks for helping me include Rosy Good of the TR Register, Steve Divall of the TR Drivers Club, Karam Ram of the British Motor Industry Heritage Trust and the National Motor Museum at Beaulieu. Extra special thanks go to Gregory Cassar, Matt White and to Soon Jung Kwon of Wilhelm Karmann GmbH.

Finally I would like to thank Rod Grainger at Veloce Publishing for his support, patience and understanding.

William Kimberley

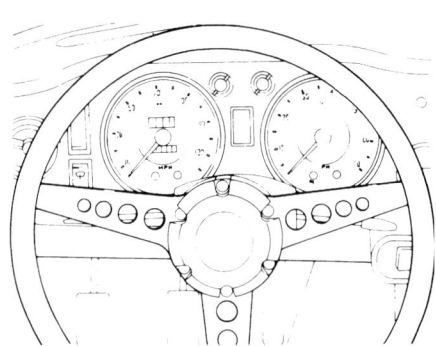

CONTENTS

ACKNOWLEDGEMENTS 4

IINTRODUCTION 6

Chapter 1   LOOKING FOR A SPORTS CAR 9
    The American market 11
    Standard buys Triumph 11
    The Triumph 1800 Roadster 12
    TRX 13
    The 20TS 14

Chapter 2   THE *HORS D'OEUVRES* 16
    Grinham & Belgrove 16
    Harry Webster 17
    The Italian Job 21
    Six pack 26

Chapter 3   "BIG MOTHER" 32
    Karmann style 32
    TR6's new features 36
    A great reception 40
    Evolution 42

Chapter 4   BUYING A TR6 56
    Bodywork 59
    Interior trim & hood 62
    Underside 63
    New chassis & body shells 72

    Engine & gearbox 75

Chapter 5   LIVING WITH A TR6 77
    Fuel injection system 77
    Gearbox 85
    Stub axles 85
    Brakes 85
    Suspension 85
    Seat belts 85
    New body shells 85
    Over 20 years with a TR6 86
    When they were new 87

Chapter 6   SO, YOU WANT TO BE A RACER? 91
    Kastner's TR 250K 91
    Racing in America 93
    Racing in Britain 95
    Tuning the TR6 95

COLOUR GALLERY 97

Chapter 7   CONCLUSIONS OF THE
              FOURTH ESTATE 126
    What they said 126
    What they say now 131

Appendix I   Specialists & clubs 133
Appendix II   Paint & trim codes 139
Appendix III   Technical specifications
              & general data 141
Appendix IV   Chassis number sequences,
              significant dates & sales
              quantities 148
Appendix V   Cox & Buckles TR register race
              championship regulations 150

GLOSSARY OF ENGLISH/AMERICAN TERMS 157

INDEX 158

INTRODUCTION

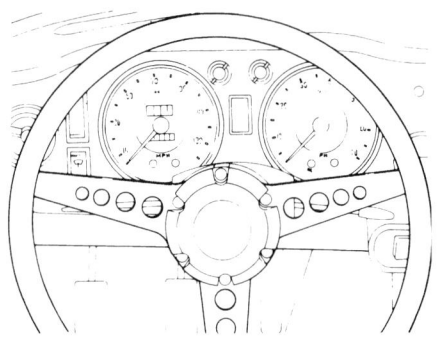

As children of the 'sixties approached driving age they were in an era when, generally, attitudes to motoring were more carefree than today. There was no need to worry about exhaust emissions or motorway speed limits, so one was spoilt for choice when it came to daydreaming about what car you were going to have at the earliest possible opportunity.

As the French master droned on,

Taking to the freeway in a CF Series TR6.

one's thoughts naturally turned to things of far greater interest and import. And top of the list was what was going to be the first car?

The fearsome AC Cobra, for instance, was an obvious candidate. It was ferocious and gorgeous, the trouble being, though, that it was completely out of reach financially. The Austin Healey, not the Sprite but the 3000, a knee-trembler of a car, also entered the equation, as did the Sunbeam Alpine Tiger and the MGC.

If you were prepared to tempt fate and empty your bank account there

7

was also a variety of Alfa Romeos to consider. Naturally, the Spiders were the most desirable, but even the coupés were enough to quicken the blood for, even when they were parked in the pub car park, they oozed sensuality. While the BMW 2002Tii was top drawer for performance, the trouble was that it was a little too boxy to appeal to the heart in the same way as the British and Italian machinery. Where the BMW scored, though, was in its engineering refinement, something that the wayward 2002 Turbo could never be accused of having.

Then there were the American muscle cars which included amongst their number the Buick Gran Sport and Skylark GS, the Chevrolet 409, Chevrolet 427 Turbo-Jet and Chevrolet Camaro Z-28, the Dodge Coronet Hemi, Charger R/T 440, 500 Hemi and the ludicrous Charger Daytona, the Ford Mustang Hi-Po 289, Shelby-Mustang GT-350 and GT-500, the Ford Fairlane Cobra 428, Torino Talladega 428 and Mustang Boss 302 and 429, the Plymouth Satellite Street Hemi, Road Runner and the incredible Road Runner Superbird and the Pontiac GTO and Firebird Trans Am. The trouble was that such machines rarely ventured away from their own turf and were a rare sight on European roads, added to which there was the usual prejudice against "yank tanks." As a serious option for a daydreaming schoolboy there was as much chance of owning one of these machines as taking Raquel Welch out to dinner.

Despite the bulldog breed British cars, the exotic Europeans and the over-the-top Americans, there was one model that stood out like a shining beacon as a viable proposition for the daydreamer - the TR6.

It touched base on all points and fitted the bill perfectly. Firstly, unlike the Dino Ferrari or Jaguar E-type, it was virtually within range of affordability and could conceivably end up outside your own flat or house. It was a convertible, unlike the Jaguar Mk IIs, and it was British, although it has to be said that perhaps that was a double-edged sword. Above all, though, it looked the part: it was butch with a capital B, or "Big Mother," as the American advertising agency bravely dubbed it, and it was the best-looking TR yet.

It seemed that as the TR range was developed the cars just got better and better. You either liked the earlier varieties or you didn't, but once Giovanni Michelotti got his hands on the TR, he transformed the model into a thing of beauty. Then came the six-cylinder engine, with the new-fangled petrol injection for Britain and Europe and with carburettors for those destined for America. The next body update was done by the Germans in the shape of Wilhelm Karmann, a makeover that cleverly blended the TR's Italianate good looks with aggressive North European overtones.

Far from being a mongrel, though, this British/German/Italian was a thoroughbred, one that appealed to the American market which recognised in it a car that hit the right buttons. Even now, coming up to 30 years after the TR made its first appearance, it's still a car to turn heads, a model to aspire to. Will the same be said of the Mazda MX5 or the MGF in the year 2020? Time will tell.

As I doze off in my dotage and daydream about my perfect classic car, the same models flick before my eyes, the same arguments still present themselves and I always arrive at the same conclusion - it has to be the Triumph TR6.

William Kimberley

LOOKING FOR A SPORTS CAR

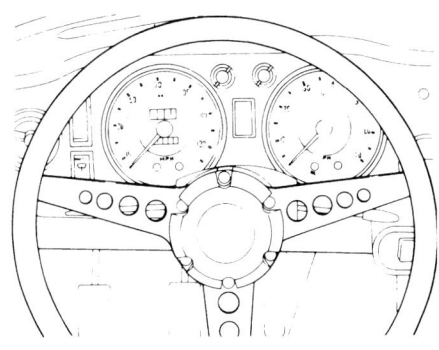

It's difficult to believe it now, but just before and just after the second World War Britain was awash with domestic car manufacturers churning out vehicles at a prodigious rate. Take 1949 as an example. The number of established manufacturers included in their number AC from Thames Ditton with a 2.0-litre saloon, Alvis with its Fourteen, Armstrong Siddeley with three models named after famous wartime aeroplanes and, of course, Austin with a host of interesting models including the new A40 Devon, the A90 Atlantic convertible, the A70 Hampshire saloon, the 4.0-litre A125 Sheerline and the A135 Princess.

Bristol had entered the fray with the 401 saloon and 402 convertible while, closer to London on the A4, Citroen was producing the Fifteen at its Slough factory. Daimler had a veritable range of cars from the Straight Eight limousine to the 2.5-litre saloon and Special Sports while its subsidiary Lanchester made the Ten.

The big boys included Ford, with the V8 Pilot and 1172cc Anglia and Prefect, the Rootes Group, with the badge-engineered Hillmans, Humbers and Sunbeam-Talbots, and Vauxhall, British outpost of the great American GM empire, with the new Wyvern and Velox models.

Sports models were produced by Frazer Nash, with its 2.0-litre sports models, the Donald Healey Motor Co., with a saloon and roadster to its name, HRG with a sports 2-seater and Jaguar with its sensational XK120, without forgetting its saloon and drophead coupe. Jensen also had its saloon and convertible, both powered by straight-eight 4-litre engines while, at the other end of the scale, was Jowett from Idle in Yorkshire with its Javelin powered by a horizontally-opposed engine.

There was Lagonda and Aston Martin, which were both owned by David Brown Tractors, the Lea-Francis with its Mark VI saloon and smart sports 2-seater, Invicta with its stylish "Black Prince" Byfleet coupé and the almost forgotten Lloyd of Grimsby with its 650 roadster.

There was also the not quite so forgotten MG, which was part of the Nuffield Organisation along with Morris, Riley and Wolseley, the ever-independent Morgan, Rolls-Royce and Bentley, with its life-saving Mark VI, and Singer which had yet to be incorporated into Rootes. Last, but not least, was Standard-Triumph, with the emphasis very much on the former.

Even then, however, the whittling down process had seen a number of companies fall by the wayside over the course of the first forty years of the century and included in their number none other than Triumph. Those that survived, however, had every reason to believe that they had the world at their feet.

The Americans were still producing cars that only the Americans liked, Europe was devastated so there was nothing especially worthwhile coming from France, Germany or Italy, and as for Japan, well, you were as likely to land a man on the moon in your lifetime than see anything of value from the land of the rising sun.

No, despite the war which had

seen the destruction of a few factories, Britain's automotive industry emerged from the ashes of war with much to look forward to. Raw material might be short, and there had to be an initial reliance on prewar designs, but at least there was some sort of industrial fabric to hold everything together.

At the same time, the industry was absolutely awash with heavyweight personalities. They might be dictatorial and tub-thumping in a way that would be impossible to consider outside a small family business today, but they had their eye on the main chance and were ready to exploit any opportunity in any place at any time. Included in their number were such names as Billy Rootes, William Lyons, Sir John Black, Leonard Lord and the Lords Austin and Nuffield. With such astute, tough-talking businessmen at the forefront, it had to be good for Great Britain Limited. Who could have foreseen, as the fog of war began to dissipate in the late Forties, that within thirty years the whole damn caboodle would come

Nowadays regarded as an interesting classic, Triumph's 1800 Roadster was not well received when new. (Courtesy Brian Long)

down round their successors heads? But that was in the future ...

The American market

As the postwar world shook itself down and started to get back into shape, it began to be obvious that the key to success, at least as far as manufactured goods were concerned, was export to the United States. It was not so much the fact that it was one of the Allies which had played such a key role in the outcome of the war, but because it was the only developed country that had remained relatively unscathed. It had not endured years of hardship under an invading army, nor were its factories bombed to smithereens. The truth of the matter was that the country's economy had remained relatively intact, which meant that its citizens were quite well off. And while the population in Britain had to endure food and clothing rations and were grateful to make ends meet on a daily basis, those on the other side of the Atlantic were beginning to clamour for things like refrigerators, television sets and cars. Not any old Dodge, Chrysler or Buick mind you, but something that little bit more exotic, that little bit special. And ever alert to such opportunities, often through their regular visits to the country, were the British car manufacturers.

Whilst those who remember or know of it now shake their head in disbelief and sadness, the Rootes Group was at the forefront of this export drive. But Lord Nuffield was not far behind, and although it was on a much smaller scale, William Lyons was also aware of the opportunities.

Standard buys Triumph

Although it is hard to credit now, the Standard Motor Company, whilst not in the same league as Austin or Morris, was still a major player. With Sir John Black at its helm, the company had come out of the Second World War in quite good shape. It had greatly expanded manufacturing capacity thanks to its government-subsidised 'shadow' factories in the general rearmament in the late Thirties, and in arriving at a deal to produce Ferguson tractors, the postwar leasehold of that extra space was already being paid for. But Sir John Black was an egotistical man. Although Standard did not have any sort of track record in producing a sports car, he was desperate to have one in the range. The notion had got under his skin even before the war when he had covetously eyed his next door neighbour in Coventry, but William Lyons was having none of it. He might be supplied with engines and a large part of the mechanical components for his luscious SS cars by Standard, but he was not interested in his company becoming anybody's subsidiary.

Then came the war and car production had to make way for things like Mosquito and Oxford aeroplanes, fuselages for Beaufighters, Hercules engines, aero-engine carburettors and other aircraft components, as well as armoured cars, vans and anything else demanded of them by the government. But Black's dream lived on and even before victory was assured, car production was again uppermost in his mind.

The financial troubles that hit fellow Coventry manufacturer Triumph in 1939, just before the war, appeared to be of little interest to anyone. It seemed to be a case of another one

11

The TRX (or Bullet); one of three prototypes produced during 1950. (Courtesy Brian Long)

biting the dust; sad from an enthusiast's point of view but great news from a rival's. Sir John Black was therefore not alone in the motor industry in showing no interest in the company. As a result the company was bought from the receiver as a bankrupt but going concern by Thomas Ward & Co. of Sheffield who, it turned out, were more interested in asset-stripping than car manufacture. They succeeded in selling off the Gloria works to H. M. Hobson (Aircraft and Motor Components) Ltd., who were fronting for the government, complete with some machine tools which had previously been used for making Triumph engines while the Clay Lane/Briton Road site was rented out for aircraft manufacture.

It was therefore something of a surprise when Black subsequently completed a volte-face and purchased what remained of Triumph from the Yorkshire company in 1944. By this time whatever part of the factory that had not been sold off had been blown to kingdom come by the *Luftwaffe*. But Sir John was not interested in real estate. Any land that came with the deal was promptly sold off at the purchase price, which meant in effect that he had bought the rights to the name and it had not cost the company a bean.

The Triumph 1800 Roadster
With everything - including the paperwork, designs, toolings and jigs - having been destroyed in the war, the first postwar Triumphs were of necessity based on Standard running gear. Sir John was determined, though, not to resort to the type of badge engineering which so afflicted the Rootes Group range of cars. In almost an early echo of the current BMW/ Rover relationship he deemed it important that Triumph and Standard retained their separate identities. Sports cars were back on the agenda and one was wanted in a hurry.

The green light was quickly given

for a sports car project to go-ahead under the direction of Frank Callaby. Having joined Standard in the early Thirties he was a senior draughtsman in the company by this time. He had never before designed a complete car; a task made infinitesimally more difficult by the need to take into consideration a few of Black's personal foibles such as incorporation of a dickey seat.

Having got a headstart on the opposition and starting with a clean sheet of paper, the end result was a disappointment and must have aggrieved Black in no small measure. While the Triumph 1800 Roadster is seen today as something of a classic, thanks in no small part to a prominent role in the TV show *Bergerac*, it was not universally admired when unveiled in March 1946. While the acrid smell of gunpowder and the dust from bombed-out buildings was still heavy in the air, most people's thoughts were not ready to turn to such hedonist things as two-seater tourers.

So, despite it being first out of the hat after the end of hostilities, there was no great demand for the car. In fact, the prewar designed Standard Flying Eights, Twelves and Fourteens, which were much more reasonably priced, outsold both the Triumph-badged Roadster and the so-called Town and Country saloon.

Even more disastrous was the fact that neither Triumph model was selling well abroad, a crucial factor in the "Export or Die" scenario of the times. Even when the 1776cc side-valve engine was replaced by the new 2088cc unit in late 1948 matters hardly improved. Of the 2000 examples made with the larger engine in 1948/49, only 184 were exported and so, from this point of view, Sir John Black's first foray into sports car production was a failure. What made it worse for him, however, was the increasing popularity of the rather outdated MG TC and the success of the new Jaguar XK120 which had now arrived on the scene.

TRX

By this time, however, work was already well underway on a successor - designated the TRX - and it fell to Walter Belgrove, Standard-Triumph's chief body engineer and stylist, to pen a new shape. Commencing work as early as 1947 it was ready for prototype build a year later with a view to announcing it at the 1949 Motor Show. The trouble was that the company commissioned to make the prototypes ran so far behind schedule that the show came and went without any sign of the cars being ready. The work was consequently brought back in-house with the model finally making its public debut at the 1950 Paris Show.

Using the Vanguard chassis as a basis, as he had been directed to do, Belgrove designed a slightly bulbous, double-skinned two-seater that, with its flowing wings, was every inch a modern car. The trouble was that it had about as much grace as a bumble bee. Aerodynamically it was ahead of its time - the headlamps were enclosed and the rear wheels were hidden behind spats - but as Ford initially found with the Sierra, what you gain in efficiency of shape you lose in customers not coming into the showroom.

Quoting a conditional selling price of £975, it was set to be the most expensive Triumph yet, which not even the addition of a number of electric gizmos could justify (these, embarrassingly, decided to burn out just as Princess Margaret was being shown over the car at Earls Court).

In contrast to the warm welcome from the motoring press, feedback from the sales frontline was less enthusiastic. It was due to this, and the fact that the revisions being carried out to the popular Standard saloons, which entailed re-tooling the bodywork, were

13

taking up all the company's resources, that the TRX was put on the back burner. There was a flicker of hope for it when Standard entered negotiations with *Carrozzeria* Touring of Milan, and then, much later, with Pininfarina about building the shell but all came to nought and the project died.

The 20TS
The next sports car to emanate from the Standard factory in Coventry was another show car. Allowed another go, as it were, but guided by Black into designing a car that would be as cheap as possible to manufacture, Belgrove's answer was the 20TS. While it showed, by being small and straightforward, that at least some lessons had been learnt at Coventry, it still fell down with regard to appearance. It was acceptable from the windscreen forward, but again it was a question of the further you went to the rear, the more unhappy it became. There were

The Standard Vanguard in 1947 guise. This was a successful model with which the TR series shares many parts.
(Courtesy Brian Long)

enough encouraging signs, though, for the green light to be given, once the tail had been elongated and tidied up, for the series production of a Triumph sports car.

At long last Sir John Black had a weapon with which to take on MG. While his new car did not ape the vintage looks of the MG TD and TF, it could hardly be called modern either once you began to peer underneath. In using the Flying Nine chassis as a basis it was using prewar technology while the half-elliptic leaf springs and lever arm shock absorbers at the rear were hardly indicative of state of the art suspension. Powered by a postwar Vanguard engine, albeit in sleeved-down form, It looked the part and fulfilled a need. More importantly it was the progenitor of one of the most loved range of sports cars which sold the world over and showed just what the British motor industry could do.

II

THE
HORS D'OEUVRES

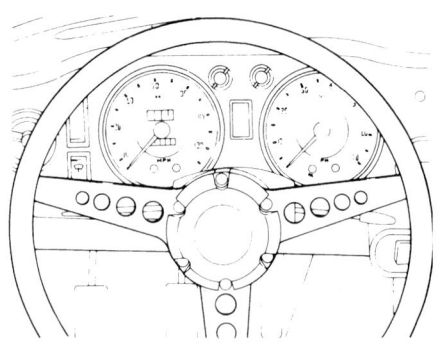

While the TR6 was an expression of a model that first saw the light of day in 1952 through a lineage that could still be traced, the progeny was a country mile away from the procreator. The original concept may have been Sir John Black's, who departed the Standard-Triumph scene very early in the TR range's evolution following a serious car accident, but its development and continued success, almost despite itself, owed much to the talent found lurking in Standard-Triumph's engineering department.

Grinham & Belgrove

Ted Grinham, the technical director, and Walter Belgrove, chief body engineer, were rivals to the marrow and about as compatible as roast beef and custard. Grinham, Standard's chief engineer since 1931, technical director five years later and deputy managing director in 1939, was a disciplinarian, orthodox to the core, unbending in his outlook and not at all interested in performance cars. Worthy but dull might sum up his engineering philosophy.

Belgrove, on the other hand, was much more of a free spirit. Having joined Triumph as a coachbuilding apprentice in the late Twenties, he had worked his way to the position of chief body engineer in 1935 with none other than Donald Healey as technical chief. He was therefore used to working on cars that were exciting and sometimes flamboyant, where looks were important and performance given a high priority.

When Belgrove and Grinham ended up working alongside each other for the same manufacturer it was obvious that it was going to lead to friction. Both were headstrong, opinionated and did not brook any criticism. Neither was prepared to concede anything to anybody, especially to one another. Somewhere in between, but really very much Grinham's man since his roots were at Standard, was Harry Webster - godfather of the TR range.

Apprenticed in 1932 he was to become assistant technical engineer even before he came out of his time in 1937. Called up to join the army on the outbreak of war a couple of years later, his immediate boss refused to sign the release papers, telling Webster in no uncertain terms just what a complete clown he was for wanting to go off. It was made clear to the young engineer that he would be providing a far more valuable service to his country if he were to remain in Coventry. His reward for staying was to be appointed deputy chief inspector.

"That was my title," Webster told me, "but, as far as my job was concerned, it really was one of the most terrific things that could have happened at that time in my life. It was because the whole factory went on to sub-contract work and my job was to sort out everything that went wrong. My remit included anything from complete aeroplanes through armoured cars to all sorts of aircraft components like Browning guns, bomb sights, bomb release mechanisms, aircraft propellers and so on."

Once hostilities came to an end

The drophead version of the Triumph Mayflower. (Courtesy Brian Long)

and things began to get back to more of an even keel, Webster again became the assistant technical engineer under the auspices of Grinham, who had spent his war years with the De Havilland Aircraft Company but had come back to Standard as technical director. On his return, though, he found a rather different company to the one that he had left and a dramatically increased workload.

Sir John's acquisition of Triumph in 1944 and his wish to develop the marque quite separately from Standard might have been good news for the purists, but the practical effects were momentous for those on the ground with their sleeves rolled up. Grinham already had his work cut out developing a postwar range of cars for Standard, added to which there was the newly won contract to manufacture tractors for Ferguson to worry about. Stir into the pot the necessity of developing a brand new, and independent, range of cars for a make that had hitherto been of little interest, and it began to be apparent that a certain amount of delegation had to be the order of the day.

While the Standard was to be the bread and butter range, Sir John had decreed from the start that Triumph was to be at the cutting edge. In a statement issued on 9th November, 1944 he announced through his press office: "The Standard Motor Co. Ltd. have purchased the Triumph Co. Ltd. Sir John Black, managing director of the Standard Co., states that after the war the experience and technique gained in the production of aircraft will be applied to the production of Triumph cars of character and distinction."

Such a scenario held little interest for Grinham. While still retaining overall responsibility he was prepared to loosen his grip just slightly, especially when it came to the sports cars Black was so keen to manufacture. Which is where Harry Webster enters the story.

Harry Webster

Initially Harry Webster had nothing to do with Triumph. His first job, once he was back in engineering, was to pore over the Ferguson drawings and patents to see if anything could be learned from them which might be used by Standard. However, as the factory began to get back into the full swing of producing cars, he found he was doing more and more work on the Triumph side.

He had an input into both the Renown and Mayflower but his real break came when Belgrove needed a chassis on which to mount a two-seater body. Little did both know it then, but the work they did during that time was to form the basis of the Triumph sports car for years to come.

"We got an old Standard chassis

from the spares department," Webster now recounts with a chuckle, "took the 2-litre engine and gearbox which we had been making for Jaguar, laid everything out on the floor, complete with Mayflower back axle, and assembled it, making modifications to the chassis where necessary."

This set the scene for what would be the hallmark of the TR range. Throughout its lifetime, even from the start, this most popular of British sports cars had to survive on shoestring development funding. Changes were generally only incorporated when they either became essential for legal or marketing reasons. "Thereafter it was a question of making the car look as

18

Ken Richardson, who had much influence on the early TRs as the chief test driver and then motorsport supremo, at the wheel of a TR2 in 1953.
(Courtesy National Motor Museum)

date it' and we did the best we could."

While budgetary constraints are the whipping post for everything, this aspect needs to be put into context with regard to Triumph and it is worthwhile hearing Webster on the subject. "I had managed to find out just what percentage of the turnover some other car manufacturers allocated to their engineering departments and submitted my findings in a report to the directors. I discovered, for example, that most German companies gave between 8 and 10 per cent to their engineering departments which was matched by only one well known British component company, also on 10 per cent of estimated turnover. However, if that turnover was greater than expected the 10 per cent was still honoured but the extra amount was devoted to research rather than to basic engineering. Austin were under half that on 4.5 per cent. In stark contrast to even this the 1.45 and 1.55 per cent allocated by Standard-Triumph was very meagre. Fortunately, though, I had some bloody good men who were dedicated to the company."

One of these was ex-BRM man Ken Richardson, who was called in at the last moment to test drive the 20TS just before it was shown publicly for the first time. A short run in the factory grounds was enough to convince him that the car's handling was a disaster and he's reputed to have reported to Ted Grinham and Sir John Black that the car was a "bloody death trap."

Richardson's opinions were not ignored: he was immediately taken on board as development engineer alongside Webster and John Turnbull, the engineer responsible for the chassis

different as possible with as little as possible effect on the tooling. Even when it got to the TR6 the instruction from the powers-that-be was 'Don't give us a big tooling bill, make it look as attractive as you possibly can and up-

The first left-hand drive TR2 prototype sporting its unique bonnet badge.
(Courtesy National Motor Museum)

design. Over the course of the next three months the team beavered away to turn what could have been an unmitigated disaster into a viable design that would go on for years. Without Richardson's input, it is fair to say that the TR2, let alone the TR6, would never have been successful.

What Standard-Triumph lacked in resources was made up for by sheer enthusiasm for the marque and an obsession to succeed. With funds being limited, though, they sometimes had to resort to tricks of the trade to ensure the model range did not fall behind. An example of this is in Triumph's adoption of the disc brake. When such brakes appeared on the TR3 in October 1956 it earned great kudos for the Coventry company for being the first British manufacturer to use them on a production car. Even then, however, it only came about by chance. As Harry Webster recounts:

It was not long before the TR2 began to acquire a sporting tradition for itself, especially as a club racer as this Brands Hatch 1955 shot shows. (Courtesy National Motor Museum)

"We were finding that the performance of the car exceeded its braking capability under certain conditions and it was causing us problems to resolve satisfactorily. It was when playing golf with his opposite number at Dunlop that Ted Grinham was told about the discs that had been used on the D-Type Jaguars and Lotus Eleven sports-racing cars. He was persuaded that, without costing too much, they would be the answer to the TR's braking problems. Dunlop subsequently granted the licence to Girling who then productionised the brakes which Triumph then used."

Initially Webster considered fitting discs on every wheel, but decided in the end that a pair on the front in tandem with 11 inch drum rears would do the trick. It also kept the total costs in check.

Important though the dynamics of the car were, it was just as vital that it looked the part and did not become dated. The trouble was that Walter Belgrove had abruptly left the company after a stormy meeting with Grinham at the 1955 Motor Show: thereby leaving a gaping hole in the styling department since there was no obvious replacement.

The Italian Job

Initially Triumph got by without a designer of Belgrove's calibre, but as the months rolled by it became apparent to everyone involved that the situation could not be allowed to drift forever. It was a chance meeting, though, that was to bring one of the most gifted Italian stylists into the manufacturer's orbit, bringing with him a freshness of line that was to revitalise the range and see it through much of the Sixties.

As Webster himself recounted to me and which he also wrote for the TR Register's TR action: "It was in the mid-Fifties, when Standard-Triumph engineering was struggling with the styling following the departure of Belgrove, that Raymond and Neville Flowers, who had been concerned with the production of the Meadows Frisky, came to see Martin Tustin, the production director, and myself about being supplied with TR chassis.

"We agreed to see them, not so much with a view to selling them chassis, but to learn in as nonchalant a way as possible more about their proposed vehicle to see if we had a direct competitor on our hands. It was during this meeting that they boasted about getting the most modern and stylish body created and made in three months at a cost of around £3,000. When we challenged this they responded by saying that within ten days they would produce half a dozen styling drawings for us.

"The upshot was that, as promised, Neville Flower duly appeared with the styling drawings and, because we liked it anyway, we chose what we thought was the most difficult one, supplied a TR chassis and waited.

"It was an intriguing project but no matter how we tried we were unable to find out who was doing it and how it was being done. The only clue we had was that there was one word on one of the drawings in Italian.

"During the next few weeks, while the car was being made, Neville Flower did all he could to get a contract on a commission basis from us, but we kept rejecting his approaches on the excuse that we had to see the finished results.

"Well within the three month dead-

Right & below: TR3s with and without wire wheels. The addition of the "egg crate" radiator grille was considered an improvement, while larger SU carburettors beneath the bonnet increased the power slightly. (Courtesy B.M.I.H.T.)

Below, right: The wider grille and headlamp treatment were the main points of difference between the 3A and the 3. (Courtesy B.M.I.H.T.)

line a vast lorry appeared at Banner Lane and disgorged the model we had chosen. It was beautifully made, exquisitely trimmed and it was a runner. We learnt from our own transport department that the delivery truck, which bore the name 'Gondrand' on the sides and tailgate, had come from Turin. A hastily organised lunch for the driver, at which he was accompanied by a foreman from the Experimental Department, elicited the information that the pick-up point had been at Vignale, the renowned coachwork company based just outside Turin.

"It was all that we needed. Martin Tustin immediately contacted them which we followed up with a visit to be warmly received by Alfredo Vignale himself. When we met his design team, we learnt that the style we had chosen had been prepared by one Giovanni Michelotti.

"Impressed with what we saw we quickly reached an agreement for Vignale to undertake all the styling and coachwork operations to our requirements as necessary from time to time. Initially this consisted of taking our existing range of vehicles and mak-

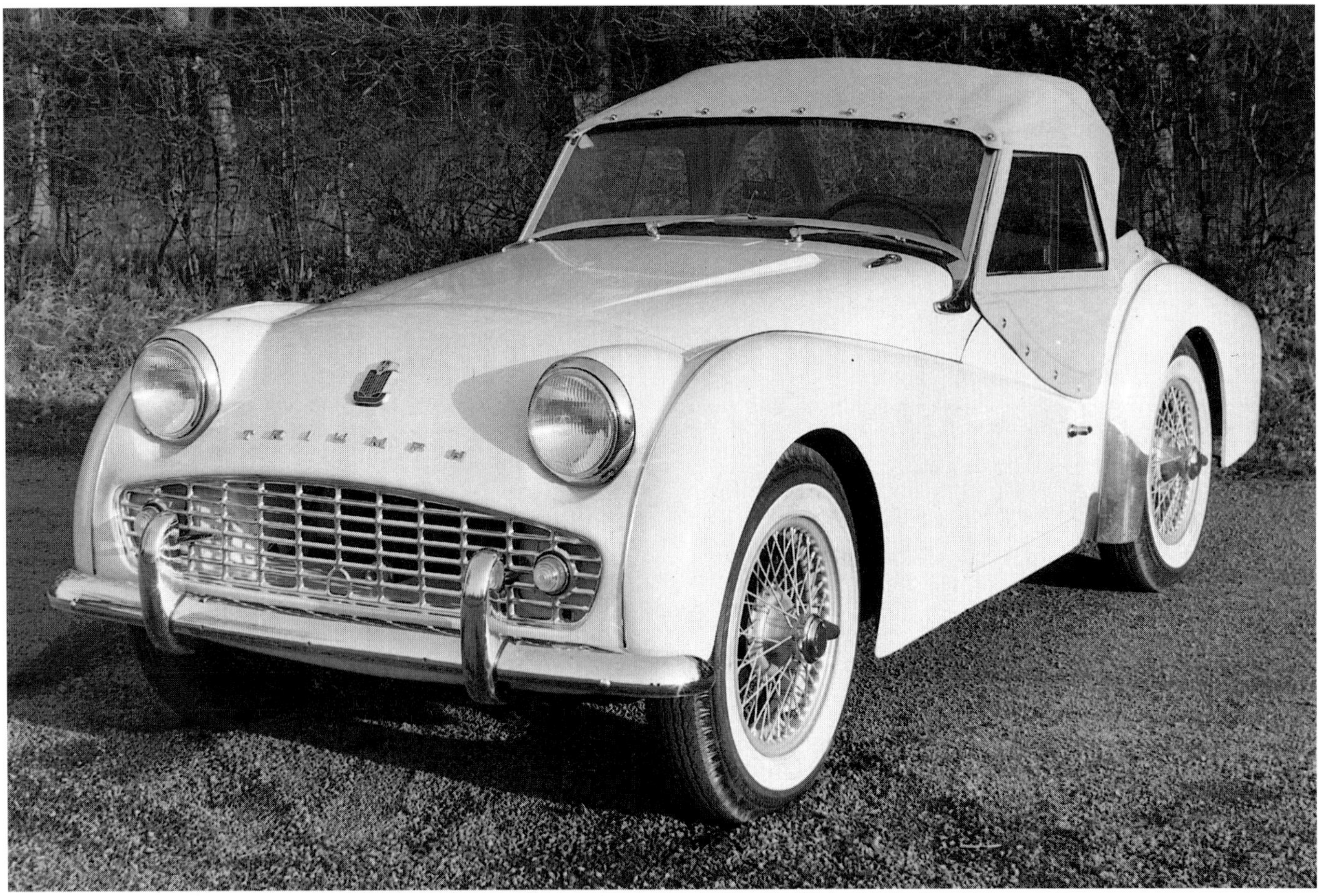

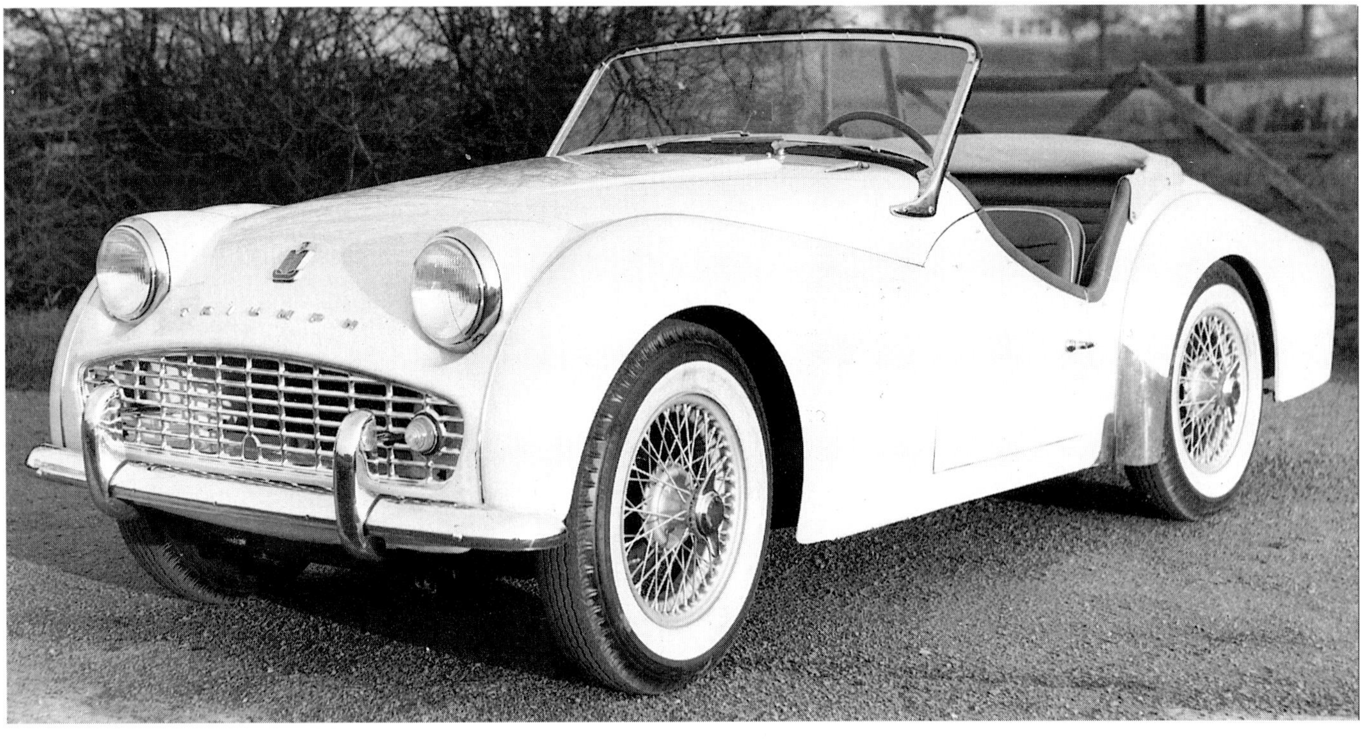

*Left, top & bottom: A left-hand drive TR3A, hood up and hood down, complete with white-wall tyres and wire wheels. These photographs were taken in 1960 when nearly 2000 cars were being built a month, most of which went to the USA.
(Courtesy National Motor Museum)*

While the works TR3s and 3As were the focus of interest in Triumph's sporting activities, they were also the mainstay for privateers in events all over the world. (Courtesy National Motor Museum)

ing minor modifications and/or additions to make them more attractive and saleable.

"When Michelotti broke away about a year later to set up his own design studio, we went with him. He had been responsible for most of the work on our cars and I had struck up a close rapport with him. His relationship with Vignale fortunately remained amicable and he had an agreement with them that they would build his prototypes."

The result of all this, as far as the TR range was concerned, was the TR4

25

which saw the light of day in 1961. At a stroke, the old car had been transformed into a glamourous and desirable new model.

The trouble was that while the TR4 did win new friends, there was a general belief among top management, including new owners Leyland Motors which had bought the troubled Standard-Triumph company at the end of 1960, that the TR range was getting past its sell-by date. The Italian styling had done a great deal for the model and given it a good boost, but there were still adverse comments about the ride and roadholding. While the subsequent chassis modifications, including the adoption of independent rear suspension in 1965, were welcomed, it was now felt that the engine was just too long in the tooth to be powering a sports car in the mid-Sixties.

Six pack

As Webster told Steven Rossi, former President of the Vintage Triumph Register and author of a book on the six-cylinder TRs: "The four cylinder was reliable enough, but big and rough. With free-standing, wet liners the TR engine block was never all that stiff. For the purpose for which it was intended it was a good conception. By the mid-1960s, though, NVH [noise, vibration, harshness] was proving a problem and proposed emission regulations would have taken much away from the old engine. We had an engine on our hands which was simply just never designed for this period in automobile development."

Left: 9132 HP. Pictured in October 1962, this is a much photographed TR4. (Courtesy National Motor Museum)

The answer was to go fishing in the parts bin and there they found the Triumph 2000's 2.0-itre six-cylinder unit. Although this dry-linered engine was hardly new and could actually be traced back to 1953 as a four cylinder unit in the Standard '8', Harry Webster's engineering boys found that not only would it withstand being stretched to 2.5 litres, it could also be fitted under the bonnet without too much disruption.

Virtually the same block as the Triumph 2000's was used (although later TR6 versions were to have a strengthening rib on the lower half of the block) giving the lie to the old argument that the TR6 block was taller than other versions.

The trouble was that despite the new engine's greater capacity, it was actually less powerful. Where the last of the TR4As produced 104bhp at 4700rpm, only 95bhp could be coaxed

5 VC during the Monte Carlo Rally. This car was one of the quartet of powder-blue works TR4s that competed in different European rallies in 1962 and 1963.

out of the six at 5000rpm. This was something like 30bhp less than was needed to make the car acceptable to the public.

The cylinder head was played around with but even an experimental one, which had better breathing at the cost of flexibility, was found to produce only 110bhp. Even though the engineering department did come up with a new 12-port head, the power target seemed unachievable without a radical - and expensive - redesign of the engine. Fortunately for the future development of the TR, Ted Grinham's huge network of contacts once again came in to play.

"Grinham had a very close relationship with Lucas," Webster told me, "and it came from there." At a stroke, Lucas fuel injection increased the six-cylinder engine's power output to 150bhp at 5500rpm and, as importantly, maximum torque from 132lb/ft to 143lb/ft at 3500rpm.

Even though the body remained exactly the same as before, including the now redundant power bulge on the bonnet, the new six cylinder car was designated the TR5 - except in the United States where it would be called the TR250.

While popular myth has it that the Environmental Protection Agency was the sole reason for the absence of the fuel injection system on cars bound for the States, it was not necessarily the whole truth. Nowadays it is an accepted fact that the only way to have an

Embargoed until October 15, 1963, this is an original press release photograph showing the Michelotti-designed hard-top TR4. (Courtesy National Motor Museum)

effective fuel management system is with fuel injection. The engine's requirements are monitored and just the right amount of fuel is squirted into each cylinder. And yet the story was circulated, and grew in currency, that it was the failure of the new system to meet the US emission requirements that were just then coming into force. While indeed the lead content of fuel is an essential ingredient as the Lucas mechanical system uses it as a lubricant for the pump, the United States was still a long way off being entirely unleaded. The real reason was that the American dealer network was simply not ready for it.

US dealers had been sitting on thousands of slow-selling TR4As for months and were desperate for a new product. Giving the TR more muscle by way of a new six cylinder engine was the answer to a prayer. However, the last thing the dealers wanted at the same time was some unproven new fuel system which nobody understood that would hardly enhance saleability. Besides, it might mean the cars being returned months, if not weeks, later by irate owners complaining about the new fuel system. No thank you!

From the North American point of view, the new six-cylinder car looked so similar to the outgoing model it was considered almost fraudulent to give it a new model number. The answer, according to Alan Millar, President of Triumph's Canadian operation, was to call it the TR250, based on the 2500cc engine capacity. The designation stuck, the car was given some cosmetic touches at the suggestion of Bruce McWilliams, the person responsible for marketing it in North America, and was launched in late 1967.

The trouble was that fitted with Zenith Stromberg 175 CDSE carburettors and a compression ratio of 8.6:1 instead of the fuel injected car's 9.5:1, the horsepower was the same as the 4A's at 104bhp at the flywheel which translated to a fairly paltry 65-70bhp at the wheels. In other words power was exactly the same as that of an early TR2: when it came to overtaking, the action almost had to be planned into the driver's diary! At least maximum torque, though, was significantly improved to 143lb/ft at 3500rpm.

Reaction to the model, however, was generally favourable with *Road & Track* reporting in December 1967 that it had a "nicely engineered engine" and was an improvement on the TR4A, while the February 1968 issue of *Road Test* magazine found the performance "considerably better than the four cylinder job." Only *Car and Driver* dis-

29

*1965. A slightly different radiator grille and the addition of sidelights to the wings differentiated the TR4A from the TR4.
(Courtesy National Motor Museum)*

*Right & below: First of the six-cylinder TRs - the TR5. Externally identical to the TR4A, apart from the new bonnet badge, it was a very different animal underneath the bonnet. Apart from the addition of two more cylinders, the engine was fuel-injected to produce 150bhp.
(Courtesy National Motor Museum, B.M.I.H.T.)*

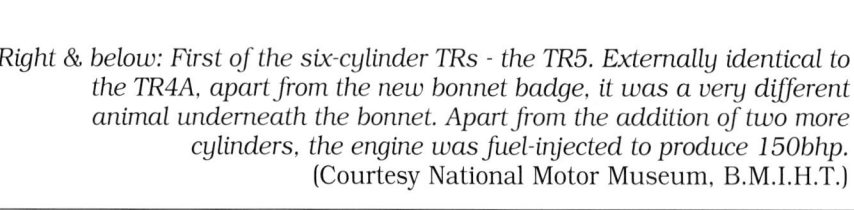

sented and in the June 1968 issue criticised it for being "a lot less fun than the TR4A."

By this time, though, it was almost a case of mission accomplished for the model. Aggressive marketing in the States had managed to shift just under 8,500 units, a considerable number compared to the final months of the 4A, and it had reawakened interest in the marque. As an *hors d'oeuvre* to whet the appetite, it had been the perfect dish.

TR6, TR5 and TR4A line up to show how the TR model evolved.

III

"BIG MOTHER"

It is freelance motoring journalist Bernard Hopfinger who can claim responsibility for the next, and most impressive, stage in the TR model range's life. In fact, his scribbling was a means of keeping himself informed of what was going on in the British motor industry as he was really the agent for German coachbuilders Wilhelm Karmann GmbH.

With a history that can be traced back to 1874, it was one of the first of the traditional coachbuilders to jump on the horseless carriage bandwagon. While the name of the early manufacturer, Durkopp, may not mean much to many, the VW Beetle certainly will, as should the VW Karmann-Ghia. Karmann also built 12M delivery vans for Ford, convertibles for Auto-Union plus work for BMW and Porsche. While the company was more or less tied to the German motor industry, it was always on the lookout for other customers and, through Herr Hopfinger, heard of Triumph's predicament.

Karmann style

As per the usual scenario, Triumph was short of cash to develop the TR range, and yet it was essential to capitalise on the six cylinder TR5/

Aerial view of Wilhelm Karmann GmbH, the German coachbuilding company reponsible for the re-design that became the TR6.

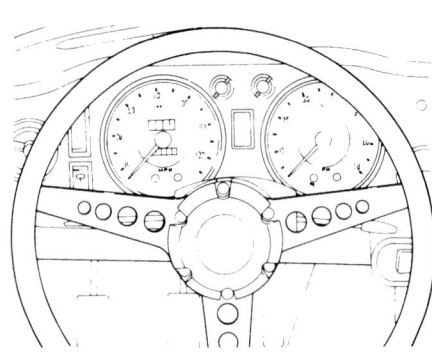

It might have been the same under the skin but, styling-wise, the new TR6 was in a different league to any of its predecessors. Its bold, masculine looks were enough to put a smile on any girl's face!
(Courtesy National Motor Museum)

Moving the headlamps further outboard gave the car a much more aggressive look.

250's success as quickly as possible. For his part Michelotti was very busy on a number of other Triumph projects and, although he had submitted a redesign of the TR5, it had not gone any further. The cost of tooling alone made it a non-starter.

Hearing of Triumph's plight Karmann reacted. "When they came to us," Webster recounted, "we pointed out that we were happy with Michelotti. They replied, however, that they were nevertheless quite prepared to do some styling on the model if they could make the tools." And that was the deal.

Realising that the British manufacturer had little to spend, Karmann kept the modifications to a minimum and left the passenger compartment, the most expensive area to re-tool, entirely alone. Nevertheless, though, they did enough to endow the car with a character quite distinct from its predecessor.

Working under the direction of Chief Engineer Rolf Peichl, Gerhart Giesecke worked miracles in the restyling. Ignoring the centre section of the car, measured from the centres of the front and rear wheelarches - to the extent that a TR4 door can be made to fit a TR6 if necessary - he concentrated on the front and rear ends.

Looking back with 20/20 vision, the styling cues seem so obvious, so straightforward, but they transformed the look and made it so much more purposeful. For a start the headlamps were moved further outboard which helped the line of the bonnet, the subsidiary lighting arrangement was tidied up and the redundant bonnet bulge eliminated.

Matching the front, the rear of the car was completely transformed. While the wider, nearly flat boot, helped by internal hinges but still with the centrally located magnetic fuel cap, reflected the shape of the bonnet, it was the treatment given to the rear panel that was most startling.

Baron Koenig-Fachsenfeld had

Not many knew what a Kamm-type tail was, they simply knew that the TR6 had one. Horizontal rear light units replaced the TR5's vertical units.

34

Another distinguishing trait of the TR6 is the egg-crate grille, the brainchild of Bruce McWilliams, Triumph's marketing man in the US.

developed the idea of a truncated rear end for aerodynamic efficiency but it was taken several stages further by Wunibald Kamm. At the time, when the rear of sports cars tended to taper down to a low point, Giesecke thought that the Kamm-type tail was an appropriate way to finish off his TR. To his and everyone's delight, it worked. While not only looking better it also increased

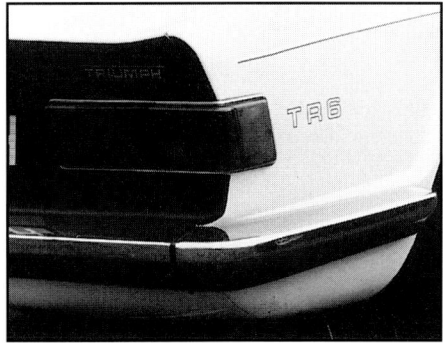

The open block lettering of the TR6 motif was another of Bruce McWilliams' ideas.

the boot space from 5.6 cubic feet to 6.1. The downside, however, was there was now a large lip to hoist heavy luggage over and to get at the spare tyre.

While this re-profiling was going on, he also took the opportunity of cleaning up the rear light cluster with a horizontal strip replacing the vertical pattern which extended round the corner of the car. The slimmer three-piece rear bumper matched that at the front but incorporated the rear number plate light and wrapped around the rear end as far as the wheelarch. There was only one maker's identification plate, in chrome lettering on a black background, which was located just below the top of the boot lid and above the right lamp cluster. For those cars not going to the United States, there was also a secondary 'Injection' badge, while on US market overdrive cars a secondary 'Overdrive' badge was fitted.

The one area where Giesecke had problems was with the radiator grille. While the overall shape was delineated by the positioning of the headlamps, front bumper and sidelights, there was considerable debate as to what to fill the void with. It was Bruce McWilliams, Triumph's marketing manager in the States, who came to the rescue with some styling cues of his own.

Taking a tip from the Italians he suggested that the grille should be a tightly patterned egg crate or 'chipcutter' style, and blacked out behind one horizontal strip, a single bar borrowed from the three-bar Vitesse as it so happens, going across the front with a new rectangular TR6 badge in the centre. It was adjudged by *Car and Driver* to be "almost to a Fiat 124 elegance."

Veering away from chrome adornments, as was the fashion in the late 1960s, McWilliams also suggested that the Kamm-type tail should be highlighted by being painted a matt black, irrespective of the body colour. His final suggestion was the use of the open block TR6 motif, similar to that found on the Pontiac GTO, on the rear flank.

When all this was put into metal, together with the blacked-out sills running the length of the car, already seen on the TR5/250 but now much longer due to the restyling, the TR6 looked a different animal. As *Car and Driver* put it: "It is surely safe to elevate the TR6 to the prestigious classification of Good Traditional Sports Car. Despite its Ital-

Original equipment Dunlop SP Sport (with Aquajet tread) on the left and Michelin XAS on the right.

35

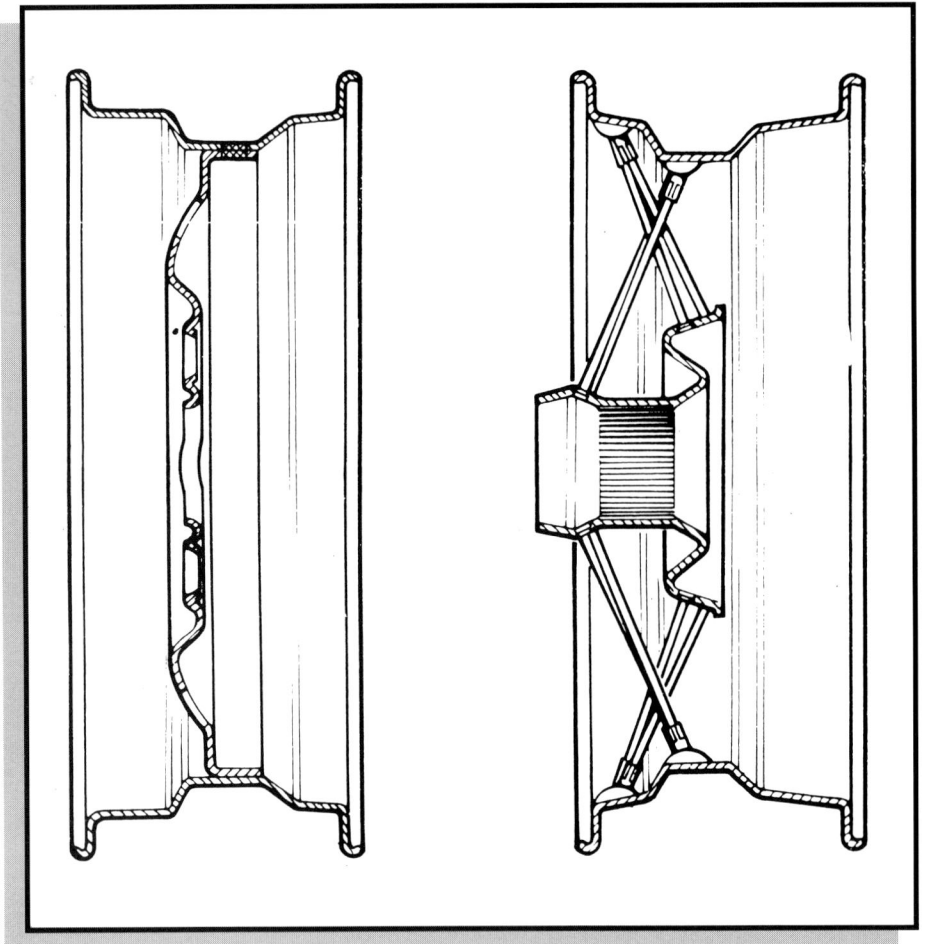

Cross-sections of standard steel and wire wheels. When refitting wire wheels make sure splines on hub and in wheel are clean and suitably lubricated. Tighten wire wheels <u>before</u> lowering vehicle to the ground

Right, top & bottom: The TR6's engine compartment always looks rather untidy, with its straggle of pipes, wires and cables. 1969 cars had chromed rocker covers, but thereafter they were painted. A seven-blade fan became eight-bladed in 1970 and then expanded to 13 blades on the 1973 models.

ian flavoured front and rear end it remains a narrow, sit-straight-up-with-the-steering-wheel-in-your-chest British sports car, but it works."

Although completed in a record-breaking fourteen months, the car's image was transformed. One of the biggest problems facing the German concern, though, was one of measurement. While the TR6 was measured in imperial units, Karmann had worked in metric. The only answer was to duplicate every scrap of paper so that there was a set in both measurements.

TR6's new features

While the imitation Rostyle wheel covers were carried over from the TR5/250, the rim width size was enlarged by half an inch to 5.5 inches. This extra inch in track gave the car even more of an aggressive look and was accommodated on the body by a slight flaring of the wheelarches. The car was shod with new Dunlop SP Sport (with Aquajet tread) 165HR or Michelin XAS tyres for all markets except the USA where they were replaced by Michelin Xs and Goodyear G800s. 72-spoke wire wheels were offered as an optional extra until May 1973 when the option was deleted.

Chassis modifications remained minor. The optional 0.625-inch anti-roll bar became standard to improve handling while the front suspension, which had been moderately stiffened in the TR5 to accept the slightly heavier six cylinder engine, continued un-changed to the fuel injected cars. That on the US spec cars, however, became softer. At the same time the swivel pin inclination was increased by half a degree to nine degrees on all TR6s although the front wheel toe-in, the camber and caster angles remained the same as on the TR5.

The gearbox remained largely un-altered throughout the model life of the TRs although it was uprated internally for both the 4 and then again to accept the increased power of the six cylinder engines. Both overdrive and non-overdrive boxes fitted to the injected cars had a 3.45:1 final drive ratio. The overall gear ratios were 10.80:1, first; 6.92:1, second; 4.59:1, third; 3.45:1, top; 2.82:1, overdrive; and 11.11:1, reverse.

Translated into road speeds with standard 165 section-tyres it worked out as 6.8mph per 1000rpm in first, 10.6mph per 1000rpm in second, 12.9mph per 1000rpm in overdrive second, 16.0mph per 1000rpm in third, 19.5mph per 1000rpm in overdrive third, 21.2mph per 1000rpm in top and 25.9mph per 1000rpm in overdrive.

The Triumph sales catalogue recommended that the maximum speeds in the intermediate gears should be 37mph in first, 58mph in second, 71mph in overdrive second, 88mph in third and 115mph in overdrive third. Top gear should see around 116mph while in overdrive it might just top 120mph.

From mid-1971, from gearbox numbers CD 51163/CC 89817 onwards, the internals from the more

37

The interior of an early car, the three-spoke black steering wheel with holes of increasing diameter towards the centre being the giveaway. Within months, this style of wheel had been replaced by one with a silver anodised finish and slots in the spokes. (Courtesy B.M.I.H.T.)

robust Stag gearbox were used with slightly wider ratios, although few noticed the difference. At 3.45:1 top gear remained the same, third became 4.78:1, second 7.25:1, first 10.33:1 and reverse 11.62:1.

The carburettored cars were slightly different again with a final drive ratio of 3.7:1. The overall gear ratios on the cars to mid-1971 were 11.61:1, first; 7.43:1, second; 4.90:1, third; 3.70:1, fourth and 11.92:1 reverse. This worked out as 20.7mph per 1000rpm in top and 25.3mph per 1000rpm in overdrive. The revised gearbox ratios from chassis CD 51163/CC 89817, still with the 3.7:1 final drive ratio, were 11.06:1 first; 7.77:1 second; 5.14 third; 3.70:1 fourth and 12.47:1 reverse.

The diaphragm spring on the clutch was strengthened on the carryover from the TR5/250 but, despite the fact that the clutch hydraulics were uprated, it was criticised for being too heavy. In a first test of the car, published in February 1969, *Road Test* magazine commented that "the hydraulic clutch takes a bit of getting used to" while *Autocar*, in its April 1969 road test, exclaimed: "The clutch took full power without slip during standing start runs, but it was extremely heavy to operate." The tester then noted: "We cannot remember when, if ever, we last had a car which sent our pressometer needle so far round the dial when measuring the effort to free the clutch. These days anything over 30lbs is beginning to qualify as heavy and the TR6 needed 67lbs."

Apart from some internal reorganisation under the bonnet, the TR6 was very similar to the TR5, even to the extent that the rocker cover continued to be chromed, although that would soon become the victim of cost cutting and be painted silver from 1970 on. The same eight-blade plastic fan was also used although it was likewise destined to be changed early in the model's life. One item that was altered, however, although there was nothing to tell the casual onlooker about it, was that cooling system pressure was increased from 7psi to 13psi. The water capacity requirement, though, remained the same at 11 pints, including heater, and the thermostat continued to be set at 82 degrees for a temperate climate and 88 degrees for a cold one.

With the exception of the silencer (which varied dependent on the destination abroad), the exhaust system on the injection cars was carried over from the TR5. Although the carburettored cars were, in time, to have the same system, in particular the four-branch type manifold feeding into twin pipes, they started out with a single exit manifold leading to a single pipe. Twin outlet pipes from the silencer, though, ensured that there were two tail pipes peeking out at the rear of the car.

The interior was generally the same as the TR5's but featured some minor improvements and incorporated most of the features required to meet American legislation. The seats were slightly modified with a deeper back for improved side support and were differentiated from the older model's by having lateral pleating perforated in Ambla material for better breathing. Initially, though, the seats were not adjustable for rake and only the American cars had the built-in headrests which slightly restricted rear vision.

While the matt wooden dashboard, "... which manages to look fake and rather cheap" according to *Sports Car World* of Australia, remained unchanged from the TR5/250, the vinyl-filled spokes of the steering wheel were replaced by unpadded racing style black ones. The rim and horn centre continued to be padded and leather-wrapped.

There were the same six white on black dials with black bezels but the rev counter sported new graphics by being shaded yellow from 5000-5500rpm, from which point there was a solid red block. The same swivelling eyeball vents were at either end of the facia and the ashtray was still on top of the scuttle. The overall look was helped by the facia screws being blacked out.

The improved sealing and sound deadening were welcomed, as was the carpeting which now even spread to the boot. If there was any problem with the interior, it was due to the original design constraints and the fact that in being rather narrow there was a tendency for the driver's and passenger's shoulders to rub together. In fact *Road Test* magazine in its review of the 1970 car was moved to say: "The driver and passenger - no pretence about a 2+2 here, thank you - are crammed in the foetal position into a space which evokes strong associations with a return to the womb."

Other refinements included a tunnel-mounted interior light which automatically lit when either door was opened, and a zip-out rear window. A number of US-bound cars were adorned with a reflective silver-grey 'Scotchbrite' striping which ran around the perimeter of the hood. While the hood was generally praised for ease and speed of erection and folding down and for being watertight, its plastic press-studs were criticised by one magazine for being too fragile.

The glovebox gained a light, as did the boot. The chromed 'T' boot handle was replaced by a chromed twist-type

Prior to 1972, seating differed between US Federal specification and injection cars for other markets in that the former had built-in headrests.

Right: Part of the TR6 production line at Speke in Liverpool (Courtesy B.M.I.H.T.)

Left & below: The zip-out rear screen is another plus in a hood which has always been highly regarded for the ease with which it can be erected and folded down.

lock with the lid slightly spring-loaded to bounce up for ease of opening. One retrograde step, however, was the omission of a driver's door mirror as a standard fitting.

For those who wanted it, Triumph produced a hardtop. This was different to the offering for TR4s and 5s in that it was not the so-called Surrey top, which long pre-dated the popular 'Targa' option, but a one-piece affair. Whilst it was trimmed and had separate rear quarter windows, and was therefore snug for winter driving, it lacked the flexibility of the Surrey top.

Initially the car was available in Damson, New White, Triumph Racing or Conifer Green, Signal Red, Jasmine Yellow and Royal Blue, complemented by a choice of four interior trim colours. Both the exterior colour schemes and the interior trims were to be widened as the TR6 matured.

A great reception
Considering the rush to bring the model to the marketplace, and the lack of resources Triumph was able to devote to it, the TR6 was a howling success. In its road test of April 1969 *Autocar* was critical of a few points, but summed up by saying: " . . . we all enjoyed driving the TR6 and reckon it to be one of the best fun cars around right now." In the vital American market *Car and Driver* stated, with almost uncanny prescience in its remarks: "The future of the British automobile in this country - we have said with some frequency - lies with the British industry's success in developing and selling luxury and sports cars. Personal cars. Cars of character and increasing refinement. It is with relief and pleasure that we commend the TR6 to your attention as just such a car." (Pity it took nearly two decades for that advice to be taken on board - *viz*. Rover). Almost as importantly, the dealers, particularly in the States, were all fired up and ready to sell the car.

Another factor in all this goodwill was the car's price. The east/west coast port of entry prices were $3275 and $3325 respectively while in Britain it cost £1020 at the time of its announcement in 1969. By the time Purchase Tax (£313) and seat belts (£6) were added it brought the total cost to £1339. Extras included wire wheels (£39), overdrive (£62), tonneau cover (£9), laminated windscreen (£9) and radio (approx. £33).

In the USA competition at the time of its launch consisted of the Chevrolet Corvair Monza convertible (which was being phased out at the turn of the decade anyway), the Corvette, which was in an altogether different ballpark, and the VW Karmann-Ghia convertible, which might not have been so expensive but was hardly a sports car either. The only true competition came from the Italians in the shape of the Alfa Romeo Spider and the Fiat 124 Spider, and from the MGB, to which the TR6 was now related since it was another arm of the British Leyland

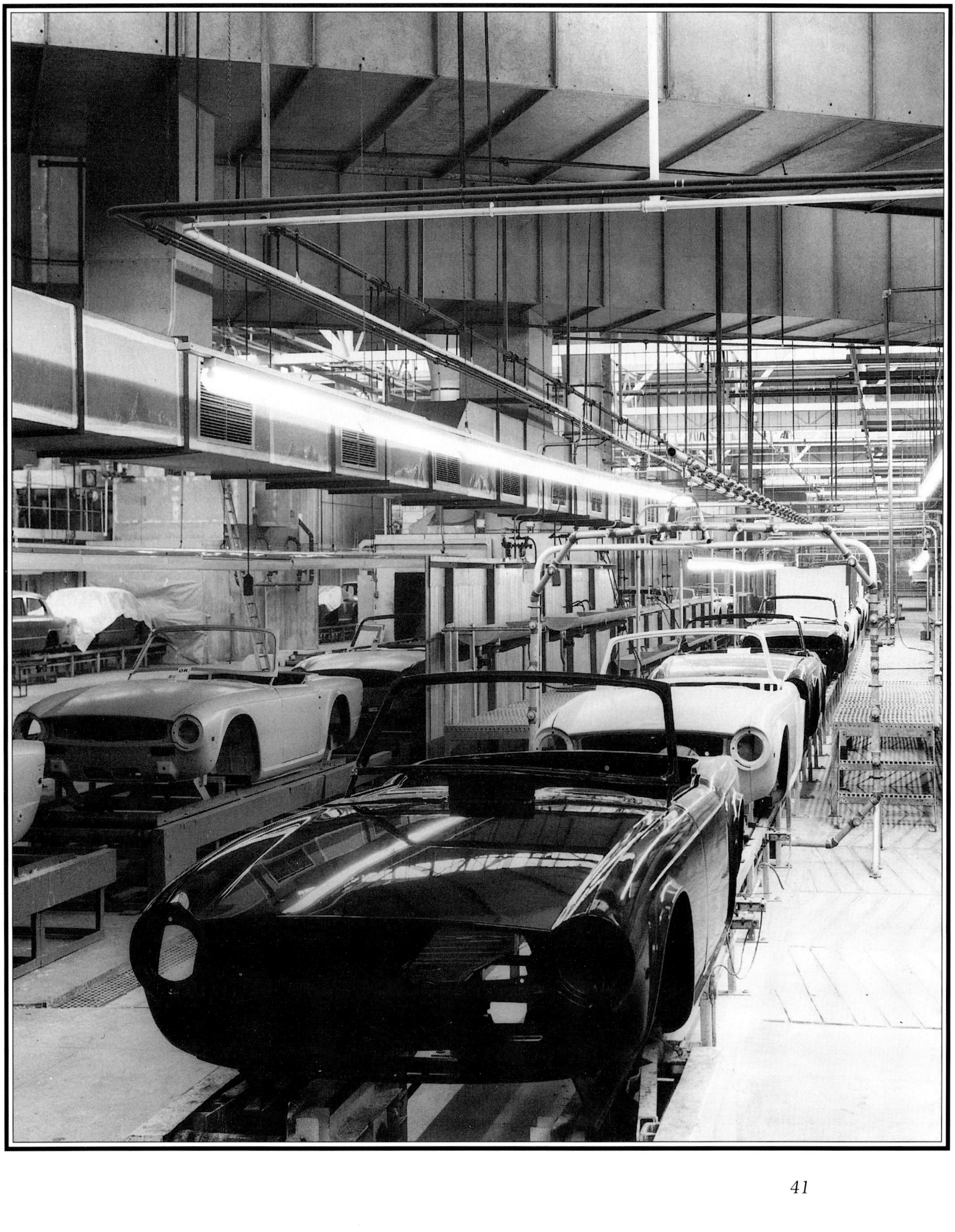

conglomerate that had come into being in January 1968.

In Britain *Motor* magazine compared the new Triumph sports car to the MGC (£1330 with overdrive), the Fiat 124 Coupe (£1,38), the Reliant Scimitar (£1482), the TVR Vixen S2 (£1487), the Morgan Plus 8 (£1507) and the Ford Escort twin-cam (£1195) (all prices including Purchase Tax) while *Autocar* included the Lotus Elan S/E and the Jaguar E-Type.

As can be seen, the only real competition, pricewise and according to the specifications, was the MGC which was £9 cheaper. Study of the performance sheets shows the two cars were very comparable. With a top speed of around 117mph the Triumph was a couple of miles per hour slower than its Abingdon rival, but in taking 8.2 (*Autocar*) and 8.5 (*Motor*) seconds to accelerate from standstill to 60mph, it was a little quicker, while in recording 22mpg (*Autocar*) and 20.8mpg (*Motor*) it was slightly more frugal. It was there, though, that the comparisons ended. Thanks to the terrible reputation the MG quickly acquired for its evil handling it was never any sort of sales threat to the TR6 and virtually disappeared without trace.

Evolution

Production of the car got underway in late 1968 with around 1500 being made before the year's end with all bar 51 being carburettor models. The first car, CP 25001, is believed to be the prototype while CP 25002 to CP 25145 were all CKD cars. The first built up car was CP 25146 built on 28th November 1968. The first car the following year, commission number CP 25159, was built on the 2nd January 1969. In this year, the first full year of production, 8685 TR6s came off the production lines, 2053 of which were the injection models.

Production of the model continued into 1970 with relatively few changes, although January saw the price increased by £25 in Britain to £1045. The despised Rostyle wheel trims were changed for smarter disc wheels with a matt black hub offset by four chromed wheel nuts and a white TR6 graphic on a red background.

The steering wheel was standardised across the range when the drilled spokes fitted to the carburettor cars were replaced by the three-spoke slotted ones used on the injection cars. Of more significance, however, was the addition of a reclining mechanism to the front seats while the head restraints on the American cars were made a little smaller. Life was also made a little more pleasant for the driver when the heavy clutch pressure was reduced by 13% by means of reducing the piston

Left: This 1970 TR6 shows the blackened Kamm-style rear end and open block lettering which were both TR6 design hallmarks.
(Courtesy National Motor Museum)

bore diameter by 0.05-inch from 0.75-inch to 0.70-inch.

Much to the dislike of the American press, however, Triumph complied with Federal requirements and relocated the ignition lock from the facia to the steering column. It also included an audible warning buzzer, a revision which did not make it to the injection cars for another year. Finally, at the wish of Bruce McWilliams, the windscreen surround became matt black.

Another concession to the Americans, this time the Californians, was the deletion of the magnetic catch on the fuel filler cap. It was replaced by a positive catch with a gasket which kept a vapour pressure of up to six pounds per square inch in the tank. This, with a recovery system, stopped vapour loss into the atmosphere. The tank itself was also slightly altered to combat the tendency of the engine cutting out through fuel surge.

It was late in 1970 that the 18-58-58-18 camshaft replaced the 10-50-50-10 on the carburettor cars and the compression ratio was reduced to a rather paltry 7.75:1. This was to meet the ever-tightening US emission requirements coming into effect in 1972. The injection cars, however, remained unchanged with the 35-65-65-35 camshaft and 9.5:1 compression ratio. While the air cleaner and assembly remained the same, the air intake manifold was revised.

In line with these relatively minor modifications was a price rise. In America the port of entry prices rose by $200 so that the TR6 now cost $3475 on the east coast and $3525 on the west. Throughout 1970 the cost in Britain remained at £1045 but in January 1971 it increased to £1111. Extra cost options included overdrive at £62 and a set of wire wheels £39 ($165 and $110 respectively in the States).

Production of the car had gathered momentum with over 12,000 examples being made in that year. Again, the carburettor cars took the lion's share with 9702 being made, compared with 2401 injection cars.

At the turn of the decade, although it was difficult to notice at the time, a sea-change was taking place in the attitude to sports cars. It was not so much that they were gas-guzzlers - that was not to happen for another few years - it was that the next generation of drivers were not quite so keen on the wind-in-the-hair type of motoring. They wanted performance, they liked to be seen in a stylish car, but if that car had a tin top, so much the better. The revolutionary Datsun 240Z fitted the bill to a tee. Little did we know it then, but this car marked the start of Japan's rise in the automotive world.

Coventry, however, was pleased with the sales performance of the TR6. It was a model that had not cost them a great deal which, in its latest guise, seemed to have gained a new lease of life. They could therefore afford to take their eye off this particular ball in order to develop a model they anticipated would be the great leap forward that would catapult them into Mercedes-Benz territory. The fact that the Stag was to end up as an expensive cul-de-sac was still in the future.

So the '71 model TR6 saw even fewer modifications than the '70 cars. As already mentioned, the injection cars received the steering lock while the recorded turning circle for all cars went up from 33 feet to 34 for some reason. Apart from a seven-blade fan replacing the eight-blade one, some slight alterations to the plumbing and a different starter motor, there was little under the bonnet to differentiate the '70/'71 model year cars.

For the eagle-eyed, though, the '71 model year US carburettor cars can be differentiated by their small reflectors underneath the rear lamp cluster, which occurred for this one model year only, and rim embellishers on the wheels.

During the year, though, and introduced without any great fanfare, were a couple of improvements, one of which addressed earlier criticisms, and the other due to Triumph making use of an economy of scale.

Rear end squat, as seen on this late US specification car, was always a problem.

The problem of rear end squat, whereby the tail of the car bobbed down as the power was applied to the rear wheels, had been a TR6 bugbear from the start. It was universally disliked and criticised but it took Triumph ages to rectify. All it took in the end was uprated coil springs and a strengthening of the trailing wishbone arm support brackets and these modifications were applied to all cars from CP 52868 on. This revision was noted by Clive Richardson, at the time Deputy Editor of *Motor Sport* magazine, who wrote in the November 1973 issue: "Another change about which Triumph have kept quiet, although this one is to the car's advantage, is rear suspension revisions which have actually improved handling tremendously. Actual details are vague, because nobody at Triumph seems to want to talk about them, but it seems that alterations have been made to the positions of the pivot points for the semi-trailing rear arms. This has removed much of the squat under power for which the TR6 was renowned."

An economy of scale modification was the introduction of the Stag gearbox (which was a modified TR6 'box anyway) to the range from chassis numbers CD 51163/CC 89817. Since the Stag 'box was designed to cope with V8 power and torque, it was an altogether stronger and smoother unit. Internally, it was fundamentally different. The thrust arrangement, for example, was more advanced with its use of roller bearings rather than the plain bush and the top hat brass bush that were used in the earlier 'boxes. Despite the new gearbox's larger layshaft and the increased robustness of the bearings on the lay gear, it was still a fundamentally poor design. All the thrust was transferred into just one area of the lay gear, causing just one bearing to take most of the stress. To rectify this problem, the load can be distributed throughout the shaft by increasing the number of bearings; though this modification is rare. It should also be noted that this is a difficult gearbox for restorers because it features a mixture of imperial and metric bearings.

Yet again the price had increased, the East coast port of entry price was $3595 while the price in Britain increased from £1111 to £1220 in January 1972. Production was slightly up on the year before with a total of 13,491

1972 saw the addition of small British Leyland motifs on the flanks. (This car also has aftermarket Union Flag badges).

44

WHP 854J, the car that featured in Custom Car's TR6 meets Capri 3000 *article in May 1972. One reviewer positively hated it: "cramped, uncomfortable, noisy" etc., etc., while the other came down in favour of the Triumph, reasoning that he could "impress all the chicks."*
(Courtesy National Motor Museum)

cars being made, 10,810 carburettor and 2681 injection.

1972 was a very quiet year for the injection cars as far as modifications and improvements were concerned. In fact the only visible change was the addition of the blue British Leyland house badge to the rear of the front wheelarch. Of little note except to the dealers at the time and the restorers today, the caliper assembly threads were changed from imperial to metric during the year.

In the USA, however, things were a little different. The emission laws were like a boa constrictor, ever tightening round the poor sports car which simply did not have the muscle to shrug it off. Triumph's Big Mother was becoming Wheezy Willy by degrees even

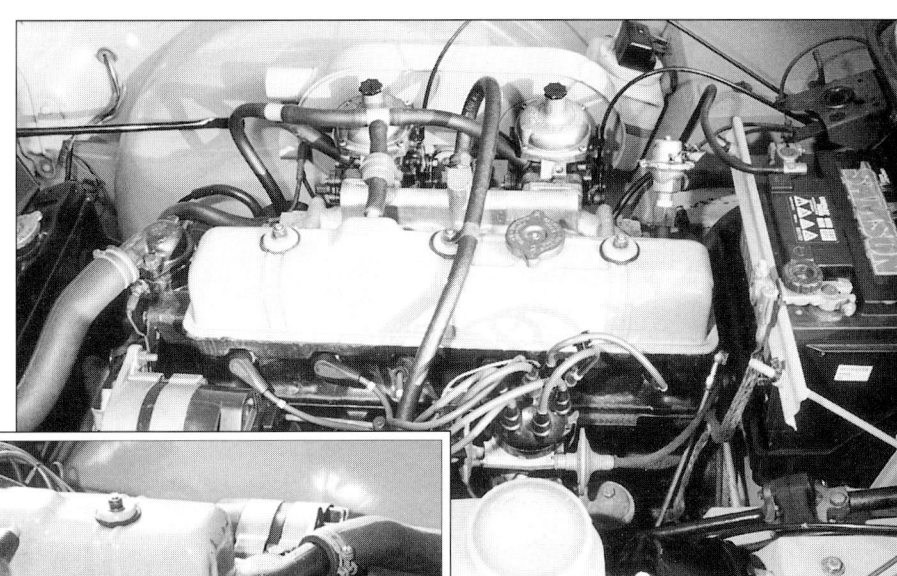

Above & left: TR6s exported to America were fitted with Stromberg carburettors. The difference in power between these and the injection models was quite substantial.

if the 185-section tyres fitted to some cars hinted otherwise. At least, though, British Leyland kept faith. Where the cost of redesigning the cars to meet the new federal specifications caused the likes of Volkswagen to withdraw its Karmann-Ghia, Volvo its 1800ES, Saab its Sonnet, Opel its GT, Jaguar its E-

Left & below: Up until late 1972 the needles of the minor dials pivotted from the top of the instrument, thereafter they pivotted from the bottom. Chrome bezels replaced black ones and the ammeter made way for a voltage indicator.

Type, Lotus its Elan and Ford the de Tomaso Pantera, British Leyland persevered with the TR6.

In order to lessen the effects of this slow strangulation, the exhaust system on the carburettor cars was modified. Although added to the cars coming down the line in August, 1971, but in fact for model year '72 models, the same twin-pipe exhaust system as that on the injection cars was now fitted to the US bound cars. This, together with a redesigned intake manifold and the replacement of the 175 CD-2SE Stromberg carburettors by 175 CD-SEVs, helped improve induction efficiency so as to maintain the power output at 106bhp at 4900rpm. Maximum torque suffered, though, and dropped to 133lb ft at 3000rpm.

Despite missing out in the performance department - the Mazda RX-2 and Datsun 240Z took 17.1 seconds and 16.1 seconds respectively to cover the quarter mile with speeds of 80.5mph and 86.5mph while the TR6 took 17.3 seconds to cover the distance at 78.6mph, as reported in the November, 1972 issue of *Car and Driver* - the car still sold well. 13,440 were made that year, of which 10,766 were the carburettor model and 2674 injection, and the dealers were selling as many as they could get.

Despite this continuing success, it did begin to become apparent that the TR6 was living on borrowed time. While there were still enough enthusiasts willing to spend around £1500 or $4000 for a traditional soft-top sports cars, the success of the 240Z in particular was the writing on the wall. Added to which not everyone would be satisfied with a car that was falling down in the performance area.

To stave off the evil day when the model would have to be laid to rest, British Leyland introduced a whole range of cosmetic changes for the model year '73 cars, or, more specifically, the CF cars in America and the CRs elsewhere. Hitherto the former had been distinguished by the CC prefix on the chassis number and the latter by the letters CP.

Perhaps the most emotive change, and the one even recognised by non-TR6 enthusiasts, was the arrival of the Union Flag on the rear flank. A clever marketing idea to celebrate the 20th year of TR production and 50 years for Triumph as a car manufacturer, it was in fact hatched up by an American, who are always far more proud and patriotic about British products than the old country anyway. It was a clever strategy and just sneaked in ahead of the time when proclaiming a car as being British was a positive turn-off from which potential buyers would run a mile.

Anyway, "Big Mother," as the American advertising called the car,

46

Not content with a "bird" in the hand, the driver of this 1972 TR6 is trying for another in the bush. His quarry is driving a fairly ancient Morris Mini Minor. (Courtesy National Motor Museum)

was suddenly draped in the British flag - and it worked. Of, perhaps, more use from a dynamic point of view, was the addition of a bib spoiler under the front bumper. This was to improve high-speed stability, and besides, it made the car look a bit more as if it belonged to the race track. The fact that only a few were ever campaigned in the heat of battle is neither here nor there, it made the car look the part.

The trouble was that under the bonnet the boffins had been at work but, while the car might have looked much more a race-bred animal, it had been in fact slightly emasculated as far as the injection cars were concerned. While the compression ratio stayed the same at 9.5:1, the wild 35-65-65-35 degree cam was replaced by a much tamer American spec 18-58-58-18 as fitted to the 2.5PI saloon. Virtually overnight the model suffered from a sudden drop in power.

It did not, however, lose a massive 25bhp as is commonly stated. The CP series output is quoted in SAE, whilst the CR series figure is shown in DIN which is a more conservative method

In late 1972 Triumph standardised the seating so that, irrespective of market, the seats were trimmed in fire-resistant material and headrests were optional.

47

The Union Flag was introduced onto the rear flanks of US-bound cars in 1973 to celebrate 20 years of the TR range and 50 years for Triumph as a car manufacturer.

The bib spoiler under the front bumper arrived on the CR/CC series cars for 1973. The roll-bar fitted to this car is non-standard.

of measurement. Therefore quoting 150bhp for the CP series and 125bhp for the CR series is not comparing like with like. In real terms the loss is less than it seems at first glance. Triumph itself used SAE for the CP series and DIN for the CR series, hence the misconception.

This emasculation was carried out in the name of expediency. The withdrawal in the UK of "5 star" 100 octane petrol at the end of 1972 was problematical for a number of manufacturers. Whilst all the new models launched during the early Seventies had engines that would run on the lower octane "4 star", those models already in the marketplace, such as the TR6, were in trouble as they had a tendency to 'pink' (pre-ignition) on anything less than high octane fuel. There was no other answer, as far as Triumph was concerned, than to detune the engine. In line with this, new exhaust valves and seats were added and some of the fuel lines were re-plumbed. The carb cars were fitted with an anti-run-on valve to avoid the after-affects of 'pinking' when switched off and a 13-blade fan superseded the 7-blade one on both models for more efficient cooling.

Ending a 20-year run for its money were changes to the unique seven-speed overdrive unit. The Laycock de Normanville 'A' type, with its overdrive available on second, third and fourth gears, was replaced by the 'J' type which operated only on third and fourth. It seems that the combination of torque and heavy-footed drivers was creating too many service problems.

Clive Richardson of *Motor Sport*, however, found a way round this, as he reported in the December 1974 issue. Having suffered innumerable problems with his car, including a broken gearbox which turned out to be virtually impossible to replace - "Triumph's pathetic excuse for non-availability: 'Oh, we've run out of spare UK specification gearboxes. The TR Centre (where the car was being repaired) should have ordered one under the US specification part number.' Perhaps The TR Centre and the various Triumph distributors they had tried were meant to be psychic?" Richardson caustically remarks. He found that, in fact, it took just a bit of rewiring of the 'J' to make it operate on second gear too. (The latter modification may not be a good idea because the 'J' unit is less strong). Nowadays, if a switch of overdrive units is contemplated, it should be borne in mind that whilst the 'A' type shared a common sump with the gearbox, the 'J' type had its own self-contained oil supply: the propshaft is the same for both units.

At this point the interior came in for some treatment, bringing it into line with the Stag. Measuring 14.5 inches in diameter, the steering wheel was now half an inch smaller and had the word Triumph inscribed across the centre boss in white. The dials themselves showed that they were now sourced from a new corporate parts bin. Surrounded by chrome bezels in place of the black ones, all the gauges sported updated graphics and now had green illumination. The yellow strip on the rev counter was deleted and the thick red band replaced by a thinner one which started at 5750rpm. The engine speed itself was shown up to 7000rpm.

The needles of the four minor dials hinged from the bottom instead of from the top and the ammeter disappeared in favour of a voltage indicator. The light switch was relocated, as was the courtesy lighting, while the knobs on the centre console had new symbols.

Cutaway view of J-type overdrive unit.

Cutaway view of A-type overdrive unit.

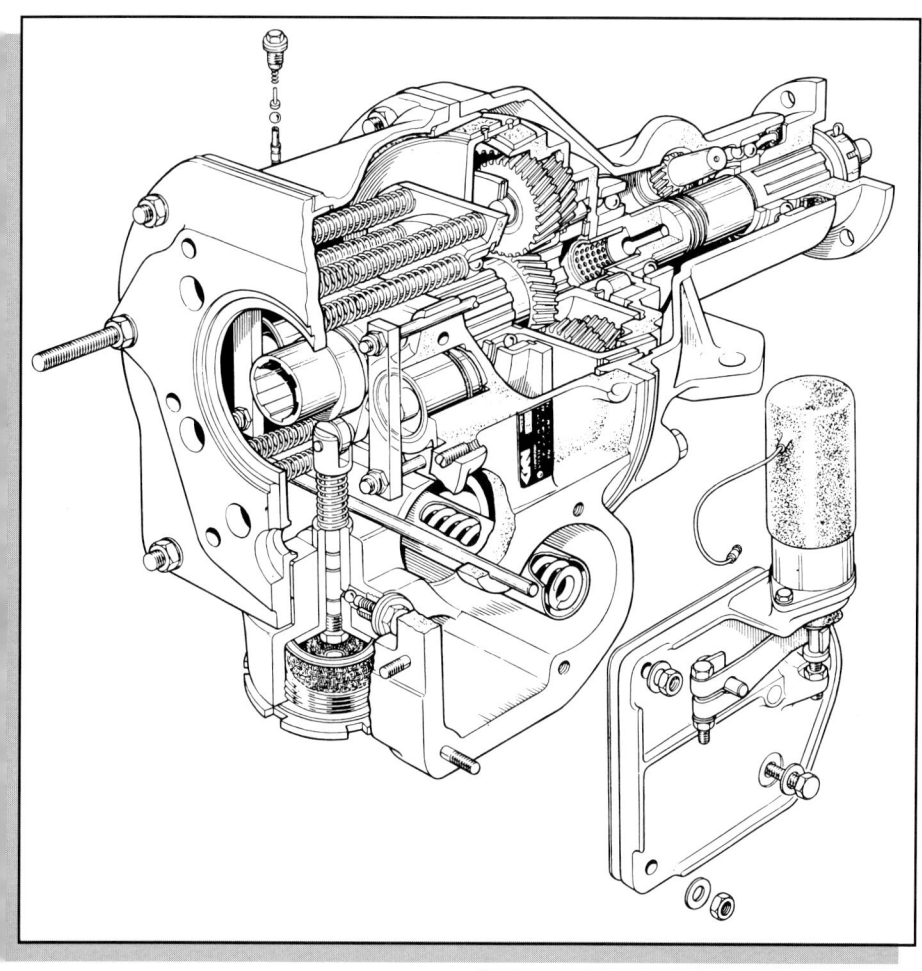

which, up until then, had always been dealt with in a rather *subsilentio* fashion by the US dealer.

Externally the black centres to the wheels were replaced by satin silver ones and chrome nuts but the 72-spoke wire wheel option was deleted mid-way through the year. The stainless steel finishing strip on the base of the radiator grille was replaced by a chrome one top and bottom and the wiper arms became black instead of satin-finished. A thicker stainless steel beading now ran along the sills.

While the anchorage points were

The foot-operated dip switch was replaced by a column-mounted one. The facia itself, though, retained its matt finish.

The seats - as was the rest of the trim - were covered in a flame-resistant, coarser grained material with a slightly different pattern to comply with safety legislation. There was a provision for headrests which were standard on the US cars but optional everywhere else, although in truth they were not very effective for the taller driver. On the other hand the new self-adjusting, single point, inertia-reel Kangol safety belts were a major improvement. In America air conditioning was offered as an after-market option which could be installed by any Triumph dealer and yet still came with full factory warranty. Likewise the hardtop

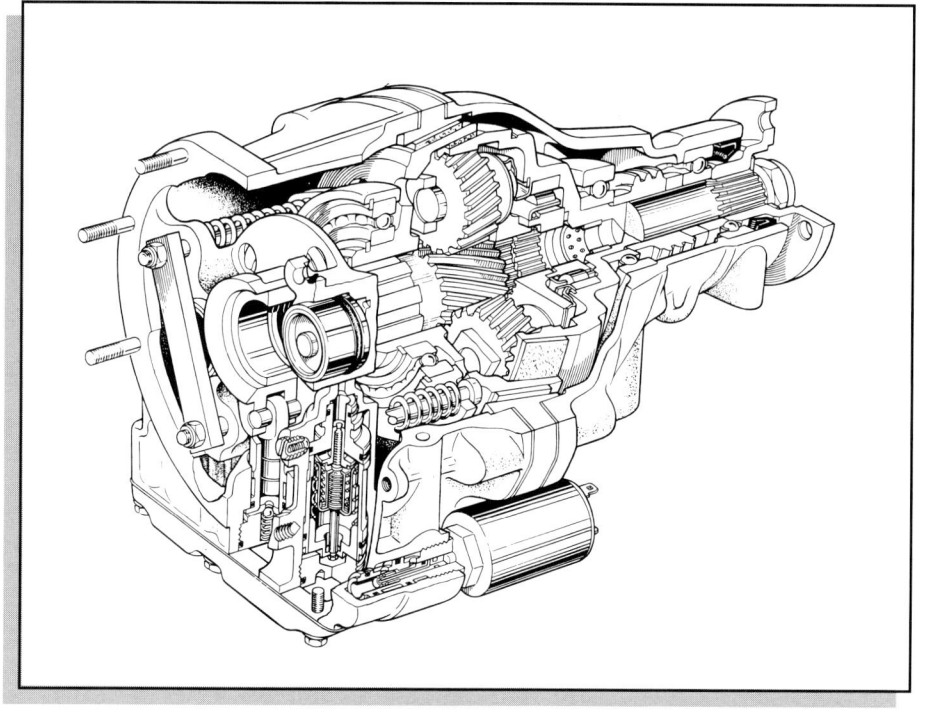

49

From 1973 the seats were upholstered in a slightly coarser material which was also fire resistant.

the same, the reversal of the mounting brackets on the front bumpers meant that they sat lower, which made them look as if they jutted further out to clear the spoiler. It was, in fact, an optical illusion! The rear ones were tidied up with the relocation of the number plate light from its chrome housing on the bumper to the underside of the number plate recess on the rear valence.

A matt black plastic ventilation flap replaced the flip-up lid on the bonnet. Not only did it look better, it was more efficient and saved damaged paintwork on badly set-up wipers which otherwise used to knock into it. Although it was only ever optional, the wing mirror - which had hitherto been the same as that fitted to the TR5 - now came from the BL corporate bin.

Despite the 1973 Arab-Israeli war, which spelt the death knell of so many cars, the TR6 still continued to sell

The Lucas Type 2M100 PE pre-engaged starter motor used from engine numbers CP53637 and CC63895.

well, both at home and abroad. In fact there were more made in 1973 than in any other year. Almost 12,000 carburettor cars came off the production line, an increase of over 1000 from the year before, while 2901 injection cars were made.

By now work on a replacement TR model was proceeding apace at Canley. The decision had been made that the new car would be a fixed head coupé, which would dispense with the TR's traditional separate chassis and be a clean break with the past. It was the bold new world of British Leyland and the result was to be the TR7, the TR6's ultimate replacement.

Even though it was still some way off from launch, it did mean that the TR6 was rather pushed to the back burner. Naturally it was not left entirely alone as it had to meet constantly changing emission and safety regulations. In particular it was the American spec cars that were most affected.

For example, nitrogen emission levels had to be reduced in 1974 which necessitated a new Exhaust Gas Recirculation system. The compression ratio was further reduced to 7.5:1 while the power output dropped to 101bhp at 4900rpm. The maximum torque was also hit so that from 1974 all the TR6 could muster was 128lb/ft at 3000rpm. At the same time the car put on a few more pounds to weigh in at 2390lbs. X-specification 175 CD-SEV Stromberg carbs were now used, complemented by Champion N12Y spark plugs which replaced the milder N9Ys.

As far as the electrics were concerned the alternator had, by this time,

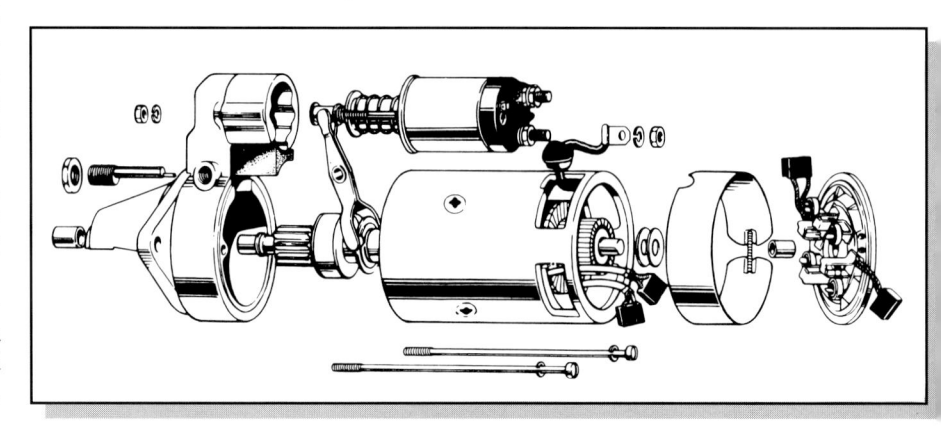

The 72-spoke wire wheel option was deleted in May 1973.

been uprated from the Lucas 17ACR to 18ACR, although some cars had an AC Delco unit, while the injection cars had seen a similar transition from 15ACR to 16ACR earlier in the model's life. The HA12 type ignition coils were also replaced at this time by the 15C6, a 6 volt coil with a ballast resistor.

Although Britain and the rest of

Below: The Union Flag rear emblem shows that this car was destined for the USA, while the rubber overriders on the bumpers denote that it is a 1974 car. 1975 model year cars had an integrated licence plate frame added to the front bumper and amber/white signal lamps fitted underneath. The silver-grey reflective taping around the hood was an option on American cars from the beginning. (Courtesy B.M.I.H.T.)

Below: The flip-up ventilator lid on the bonnet was replaced in 1973 with a black plastic grille.

Above & right: 1974 right-hand drive TR6 sporting a black plastic air dam under the front bumper and silver centres to the wheels.

the world was similarly affected, the USA was blighted by safety legislation which required that the safety belts be buckled up before the engine could be started. This was enforced by a seat sensor which, upon detecting a person's weight, would only allow the car to start once the belt had been buckled. It caused such a considerable outcry in the USA at the time that within the year the requirement was dropped. For that year, though, the TR6, like every other car on the American market at that time, had the device fitted.

Another unfortunate development was the addition of new rubber overriders, or 'tits', as they were colloquially known, to the bumpers front and rear. Thanks to some bright spark reading the fine print of the legislation, they were the lesser of two evils. While the bumpers had to withstand a 5mph impact without any damage to the lights, a proviso in the law, aimed specifically at the smaller manufacturer, negated the necessity to redesign the entire bumper as long as there were some bumperettes. It was a point missed by Alfa Romeo, BMW, Fiat and poor old MG who set about adorning their models with the most hideous designs, much to the detriment of overall appearance.

The new US minimum bumper height requirement was met by shimming the front springs around an inch, but it was to the detriment of the handling and, in widespread acts of covert civil disobedience, most owners set about dumping the shims as soon as they knew how!

Door pulls that were integrated into the side panel, a telescopic aerial and twin speakers on each side of the console now became standard on the carburettor cars, but the writing was on the wall for the injection cars. One month after the TR7 was announced in America the last fuel injected TR6 trundled down the production line.

Altogether 13,912 examples were made, most in Coventry but a few of the early cars were assembled from Completely Knocked Down (CKD) kits in Belgium. A total of 8370 was sold in the UK with 5500 exported to Europe and Australasia. 1973 was the best year for domestic sales with 1948 examples sold but which more than halved the following year when sales reached just 843. Despite the last car being built in February, the downturn in sales meant that there were 545 registered sales that year and a further 14 in 1976.

While the model was dying a slow death back home, it continued to sell quite well in the States. In fact 1974 proved to be the best year ever for the TR6 with 13,740 sold, up 2035 on the

53

Huge rubber overriders were an affliction on late model TR6s bound for the USA.

year before. Naturally the advent of the TR7 dented demand quite considerably in 1975, but sales were still quite a healthy 9228 and only slightly less at 7208 in 1976, its final year of production, although like the UK, sales would trickle into the next year with 146 TR6s recorded as having been sold.

Bit by bit the car put on weight to become 2390lbs in 1975 and 2410 lbs in 1976 but it differed very little externally. Now that production was devoted to the American market, the front bumper was designed to accept the American licence plate. The amber/white signal lights that sprouted on the car beneath the front bumper at either end in 1975 were changed for amber/amber the following year.

It was the last of the dinosaurs. Air conditioning, concerns about safety and the probable outlawing of open topped cars led to the TR6's demise. Whoever wanted to feel the wind rushing through their hair when they could drive around in the cossetted comfort of a mobile sitting room? Open sports cars were outmoded, unfashionable and anti-social. Good riddance to the anachronistic pieces of metal. The open-topped two-seater sports car was dead, never to be revived, consigned to the dustbin of history.

We were now in the era of the hot hatch. Long live the Golf GTI which had just been born in Germany. Hail the conquering 205GTI from France! More power to the Ford Escort XR3i - Essex man's answer to the yob culture that was about to engulf Western society in the 1980s. Except that as sure as night follows day, the wheel of fashion has gone full circle.

The hot hatch is now in its death throes, manufacturers just cannot bring out their two-seater sports cars quick enough and even Rover is getting in on the act. True, neither the MGR V8 nor the new MGF model will carry the Triumph badge, but they are the spiritual successor to the TR range of cars that so successfully carried the Coventry name around the world.

Nothing can diminish the fact that the 6 was the most successful TR up to that time. Between 1969-1975 almost 95,000 examples were made. It was a natural successor to the Austin-Healey 3000, it outshone the lacklustre MGC and it was substantially cheaper than the Jaguar E-Type. In its injection form it was the definitive open topped muscle car in an era that worshipped brawn.

Another 1974 TR6, this time with hardtop in place.

IV

BUYING
A
TR6

TRIUMPH TR6. 1972. Original RHD, red. Recent mechanical overhaul. £xxxx. Or TRIUMPH TR6, Mimosa yellow. 72,000 miles. One previous owner, taxed, new hood and tonneau. Red band tyres, sound original order. Beautiful condition. Garaged. £xxxx. Or TRIUMPH TR6. Unfinished project needing restoration, bodywork partly restored and reconditioned gearbox. £xxxx.

How beguiling! It's Spring and you're in the mood for a spot of open air motoring. You've got a bit of money to spend and you really fancy one of Triumph's best. But it's a daunting task. You are going to buy a car that has to be at least 21 years old if you're in Britain and may be up to 26 years old. Should you go for the car that's recently been overhauled, or possibly the completely original one that has been garaged or should you plump for the unfinished project? Maybe you could buy one that has spent its life in the USA? Nothing can beat the rust-free environment of California or Arizona. What happens, though, if it was a New England car? It might just as well have spent its life in Grimsby!

Much, of course, will depend on your circumstances. If you are an enthusiast who just wants to get into a car and drive off into the sunset, the answer is probably none of the above. Wisdom dictates that you will be looking for the nut and bolt restoration and, of course, you will want to see documentary proof of this. Photographs

While it's hard to beat the rust-free environment of Arizona, not all American cars went to that state and were, therefore, often just as prone to the ravages of rust as if they had stayed in Britain.

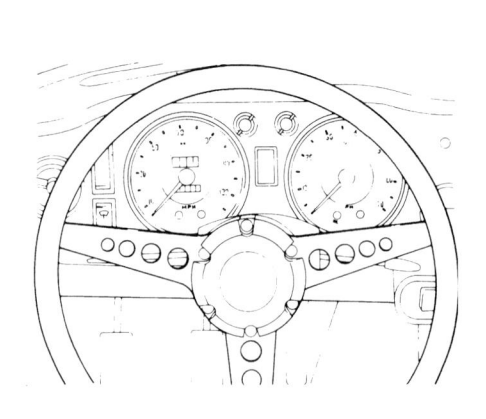

Some prefer to go for a car which requires a ground-up restoration: at least they can then be sure the finished car will be totally sound, with no hidden surprises.

taken while the car was being restored, invoices for the parts supplied new, the names of the suppliers and so on. Naturally, you will be paying top drawer prices for this privilege, so you will want to be assured that the car is perfect in every way.

The unfinished project is at the other end of the scale. The beauty of it is that the initial outlay will not be too high but, ultimately, you will still need deep pockets. You will also get to know one or more of the specialists so intimately that about the only thing you won't know is their hat size.

The knowledge and services that specialists can provide you will, however, find invaluable. Long gone are the days when you had to scour junk yards for a bootlid, spoiler or front headlamp. More or less every panel is available off the shelf, all shiny and new. Apart from the bulkhead section itself there is nothing that cannot be replaced in an original shell. You can,

Today, pretty well every part of a TR6 is available off the shelf. Until 1992 rear light lenses, for example, were like gold dust but have since become widely available, thanks to a specialist company that manufactures them.

for example, cut out all the rot and replace the floorpans and the inner and outer sills. You can rehabilitate the decks, wings, inner wings and wheelarches. You can even go out and buy a brand new shell and chassis if

Above & below: 'Do all the panels fit properly?' One of the questions you should be asking yourself when buying a car you do not intend to restore. This American example looks good, but was later subject to a ground-up restoration.
(Courtesy Gregory Cassar)

The car should sit squarely on the ground. Drooping corners indicate trouble in store.
(Courtesy Gregory Cassar)

you are so inclined. What you will need, however, are metal skills beyond the average DIY enthusiast.

Even minor parts are available. Until 1992, for example, rear light lenses were like gold dust and led to some owners being tempted to sell their grandmothers to get a pair. Moss Europe, one of the leading classic car specialists, became aware of the situation and set about re-manufacturing them on original equipment tooling, while ensuring at the same time that they complied with the appropriate European and DoT requirements.

The alternative to all this, of course, is to commission a specialist company to build you a better than new vehicle. However, for a blank sheet of paper job, be prepared to spend at least double the usual asking price for a very good TR6: it's also an investment you are unlikely, ever, to see returned if the car has to be sold, but then, of course, you should be comparing the outlay to the price of a new car.

The specialists will sell you manuals on how to assemble the car and fit the parts; they are generally helpful at the end of the telephone, to a point, and few are the problems that they have not encountered before. Then there are always the clubs, the source of so much knowledge and help that becoming a member should be a prerequisite for owning a TR6.

The car that is the real gamble and a pig in the poke to buy is the "one owner since new, very original." On the one hand it can be just that. It may have been loved and cherished all its life, garaged and well looked after. On the other hand it can be an epithet for a disaster area. Superficially alright, it may have suffered from neglect and ill treatment. A glance at the servicing records will give you some sort of indication, but you will still need to pay close attention to the condition.

Bodywork

"The first thing we look at when we look at a sale car," Darryl Uprichard of Racetorations, one of the premier TR specialists, commented, "is whether all the panels fit and if they don't, why not? Was it in an accident, or was it another rebuild? It can be all sorts of things." It is worth pointing out, though, that Triumph itself sometimes had trouble with panel fit on the production line. It is rumoured that if they could not achieve continuity along the swage lines on the side of the car, lead filler would be applied on the offending panel until it matched its neighbours.

From a distance run your eye down each side of the car. There are almost always a few ripples but look for signs of poor workmanship where there have been repairs. See if the car sits on the ground squarely and ensure that the wheels sit centrally in the wheelarches. If they do not it could mean a number of things, most of them expensive to rectify. It could, for example, mean that the suspension is damaged (of which more anon) or it might even mean that the car has been involved in an accident and the chassis is out of true.

Closely examine the shutlines. Even when new some were far from perfect, especially the gap around the doors, but the trailing edge of a door should not overlap the wing as has been known to happen. If you are interested in entering concours events with your new purchase, don't buy one with glassfibre wings: they don't affect the structural integrity of the car, but will lose you points on originality.

Although the body is a fairly simple affair and has the advantage of having a separate chassis, there are a number of rust traps which need checking. One, for example, is around the headlamps. Mud becomes trapped above the bowl from where the rust spreads around the lamp and through the front wing.

While peering under the bonnet check the area around the battery box and by the brake and clutch cylinders. The front panel and valance can survive the ravages of time remarkably well but they are regarded as well known danger spots and so need examining quite closely.

The inner wings need to be checked over very carefully, from inside and out, as they need to be in good condition to be mated to a new outer wing if that needs replacing. In fact, any accident damage is more likely to be spotted by peering from under the bonnet than from the outside. Although it is not a well known fact, the petrol injection cars had a slightly differently contoured offside wheelarch to the carburettor cars and, at the time of writing, such panels are unavailable new.

The rear inner wings are also susceptible to the dreaded red menace due to the mud and water thrown up by the rear tyres. Carefully examine for bubbling the area above the tail lights, which was vulnerable due to the difficulty of undersealing that section, and along the edge closest to the door.

The bottom of the doors need inspecting since the drain holes have a tendency to become blocked by debris, water trapped in the doors leads to serious corrosion.

The body around the B posts needs to be checked because this is an expensive to repair. It's another weak part of the car which, due to the design, has encouraged sweating. In other words it is where water has worked its way into the area due to capillary action and has then become trapped to work its evil ways.

The rear deck is made out of just one section and is at its weakest where it joins the inner and outer wings due, again, to sweating. As it corrodes it tends to become separated from the wings.

Open the boot and check from the inside. While in there remove the interior trim to check the floor around the bottom of each wheelarch for rust and have a look along the leading edge of the bootlid. Ensure that the spare wheel is there, that it is not sitting in a pool of water, and that it matches the other four. The lid itself can rot where the inner and outer panels join each other at the rear edge.

The lower inner rear valance panel has a tendency to rust due to becoming clogged with mud and the sills are prone to rot. They are of an intricate

Left & below: Under the bonnet inspect the area around the battery and the brake and clutch master cylinders very carefully. (Courtesy Gregory Cassar)

construction and in fact consist of a small inner section, which is hidden from view, an outer section and a third piece where the floor panel is folded over. It's therefore quite an involved operation to bring them back to par and necessitates taking off the front and rear wings to replace them. Beware, though, of the car which has had a second set of sills fitted over the original. While superficially they may look alright, they could be hiding a can of worms and in a worst case scenario be offering no structural support to the body. The only thing to do is to replace everything.

One particular area to check out is the front end of the sill just behind the wheelarch. The scuttle has a rubber tube to direct any water safely out of harm's way. Unfortunately, though, it has a tendency to become blocked at the bottom and so becomes the starting point of a serious rust trap.

Another weak area, in which problems are often caused by neglect, is the bottom of the windscreen frame and

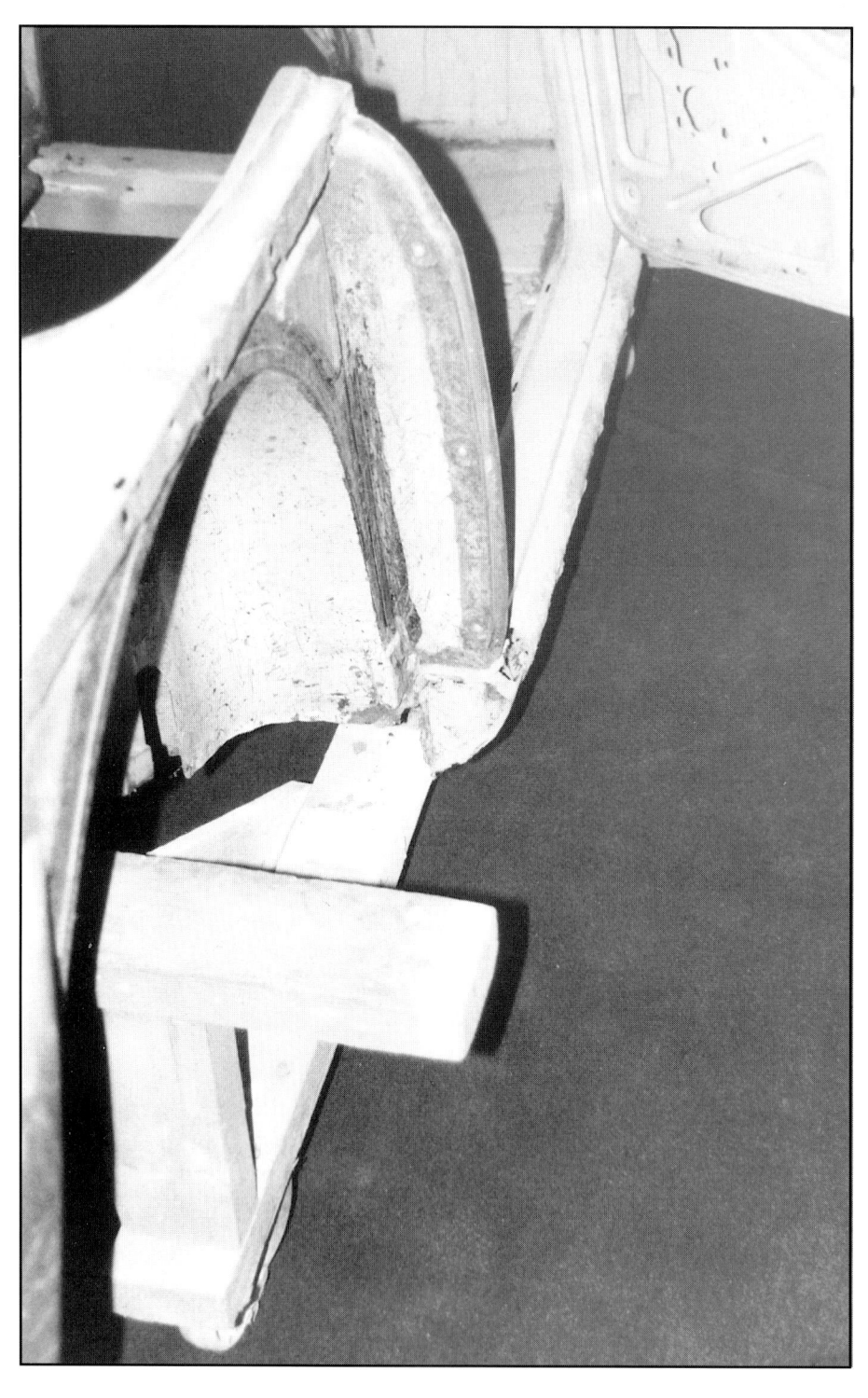

The inner wings need to be in good condition for structural strength and to ensure the outer wing fits properly.

Right: The rear inner wings are prone to rust, especially where panels overlap or join.

inside the scuttle itself. This occurs when undetected leaves worm their way into the ventilation flap and then clog the system. Trapped water then proceeds to do its worst.

Interior trim & hood

Inside the car have a good peer around. Lift up the carpet and check integrity of the inner sills. If they need replacing, so will the outer ones, and, as already explained, that is a major job.

Whether you want the TR for the sheer joy of owning one, or have concours ambitions, will dictate how you view the trim. If you are in the concours category, it will be essential that the trim matches the year of the car. As the car evolved it was subject to a number of different designs and a wrong pattern for a given year will cost you points. Even if you are not preoccupied with such thoughts, you'll still want to check that the seat frames are not broken, that the seat runners are fastened to the floor, that the carpets are in good shape and that the soft moulded trim is in place. All these parts, except the seat runners, are readily available from specialists, but they are expensive and so need to be taken into account in the price of the car.

Structurally the interior should be perfect, but check the floorpan and footwells and ensure that the strong aluminium H panel which houses the radio is in place. It gives the dashboard structural integrity and eliminates scuttle shake allowing the instruments to be read. The wood veneer of the dashboard is also liable to crack due to wear and tear; although this item is easily replaceable, it is nevertheless another expense.

There's little to go wrong with the hood, which may be torn or the rear screen scratched, but such items are replaceable, at a price, if necessary. Ensure the hood frame is in good working order and that there is a frame if buying a hard top.

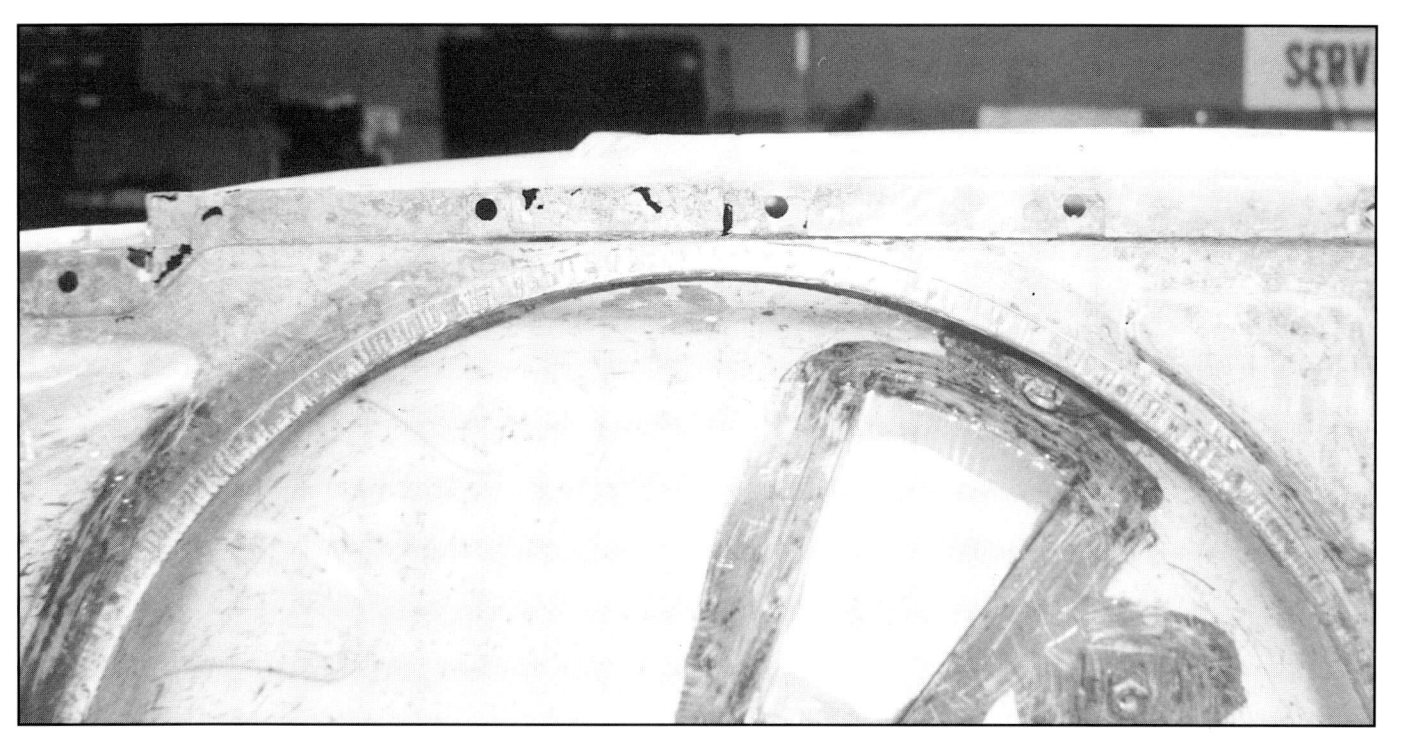

Underside

The next stage is to look underneath the car. Although this is very difficult without putting the car up on a ramp, it is definitely worthwhile having a good poke around. One of the saving graces of the car was that it was built with a proper chassis which gives it an inert strength.

A huge problem area on the chassis is around the differential bridge area. The whole back end of the TR6, from behind the driver's backside to behind the rear wheels, is usually rotten so every car inspected should be

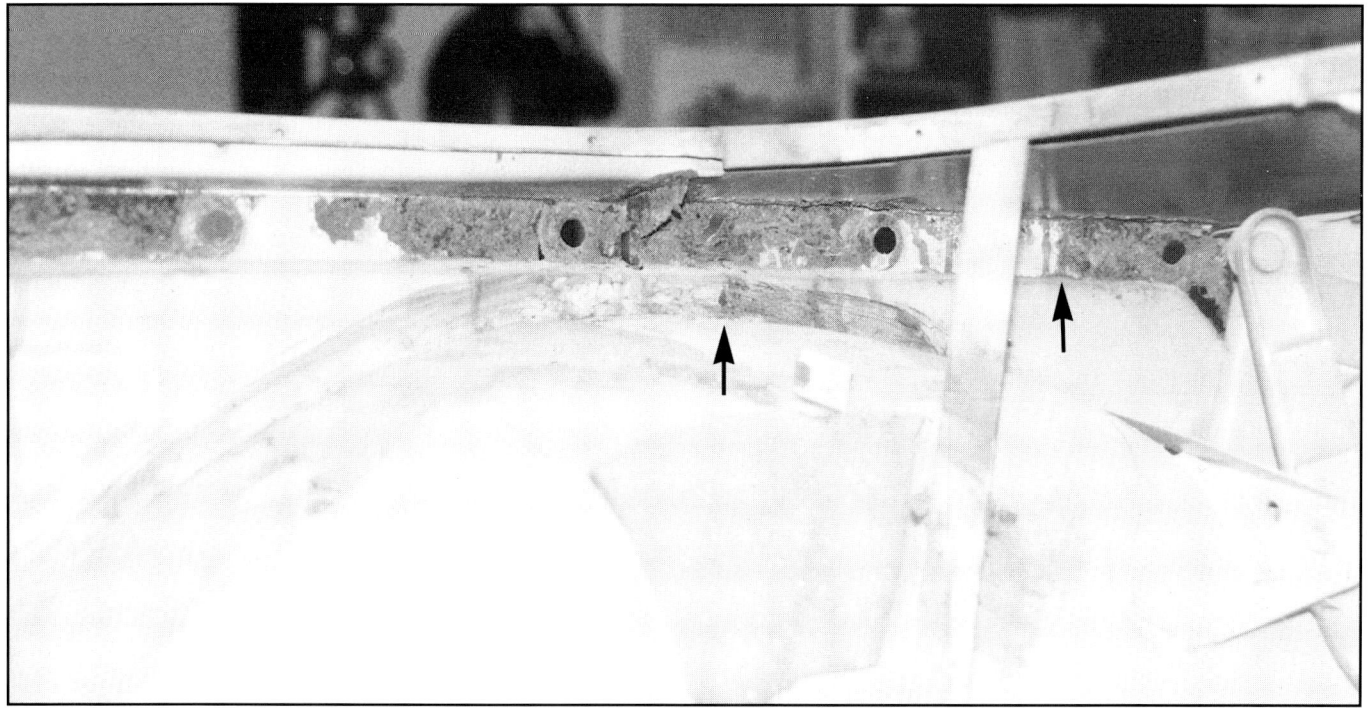

The rear deck is weakest where it joins the outer and inner wings.

In the rear section of the cockpit and in the boot all the seams are prone to rust (here the rear deck has been removed).
(Courtesy Gregory Cassar)

The inner door post areas, which are hidden from the eye, have a tendency to rust, as does the floorpan which is being cut out in this car.
(Courtesy Gregory Cassar)

64

One area to check for rust is the front end of the sill at the back of the door post.

Blockage of the drain tubes can lead to the area around the base of the windscreen becoming rotten.
(Courtesy Gregory Cassar)

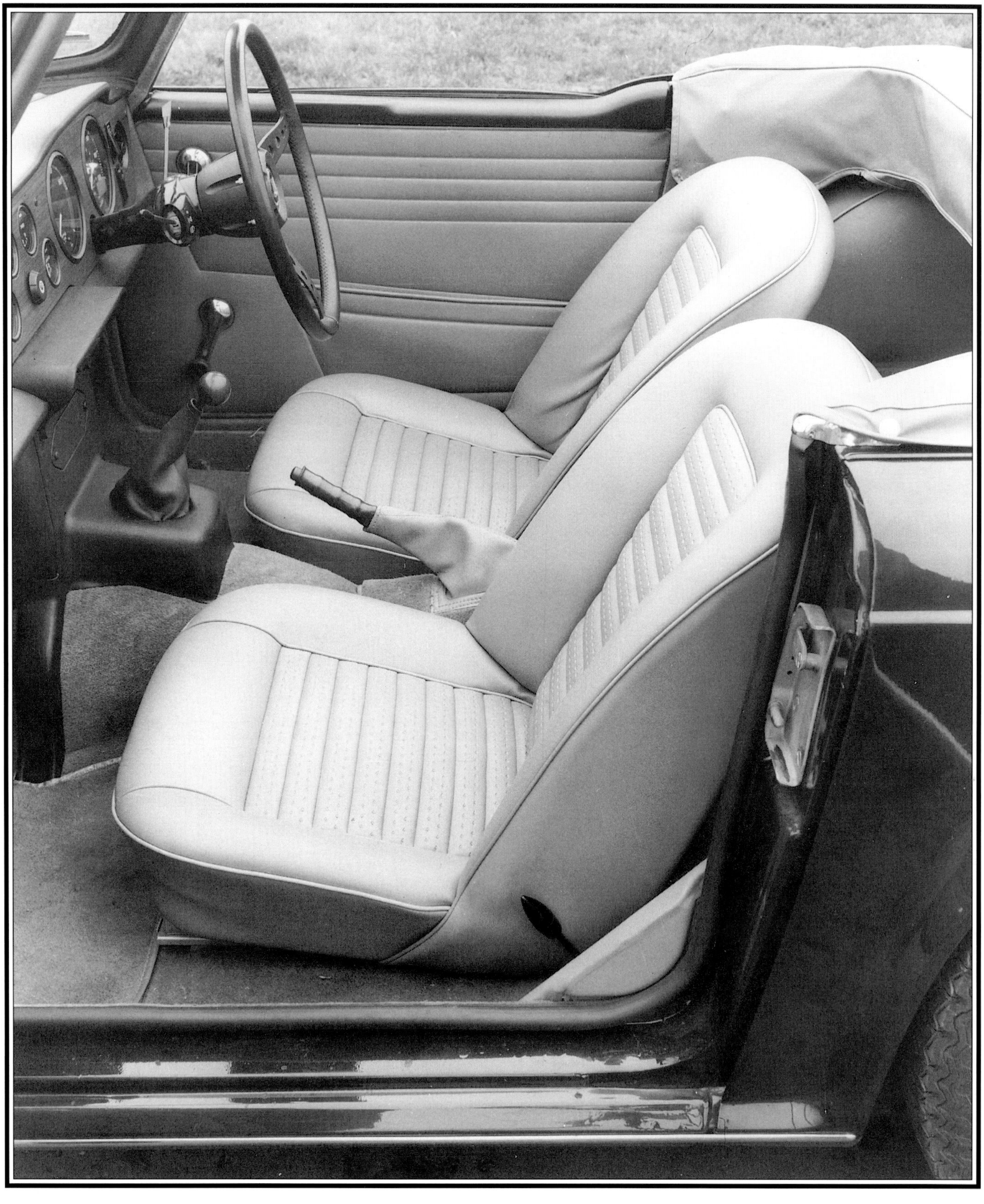

Left: Interior trim should be in good condition, like this early car's, and of correct specification for the year of the car.

Rusted floorpans are a common problem. The solution is to cut out the old panel ...

... repair, clean and paint the chassis beneath ...

... repair adjacent areas of bodywork, like the toe board shown here ...

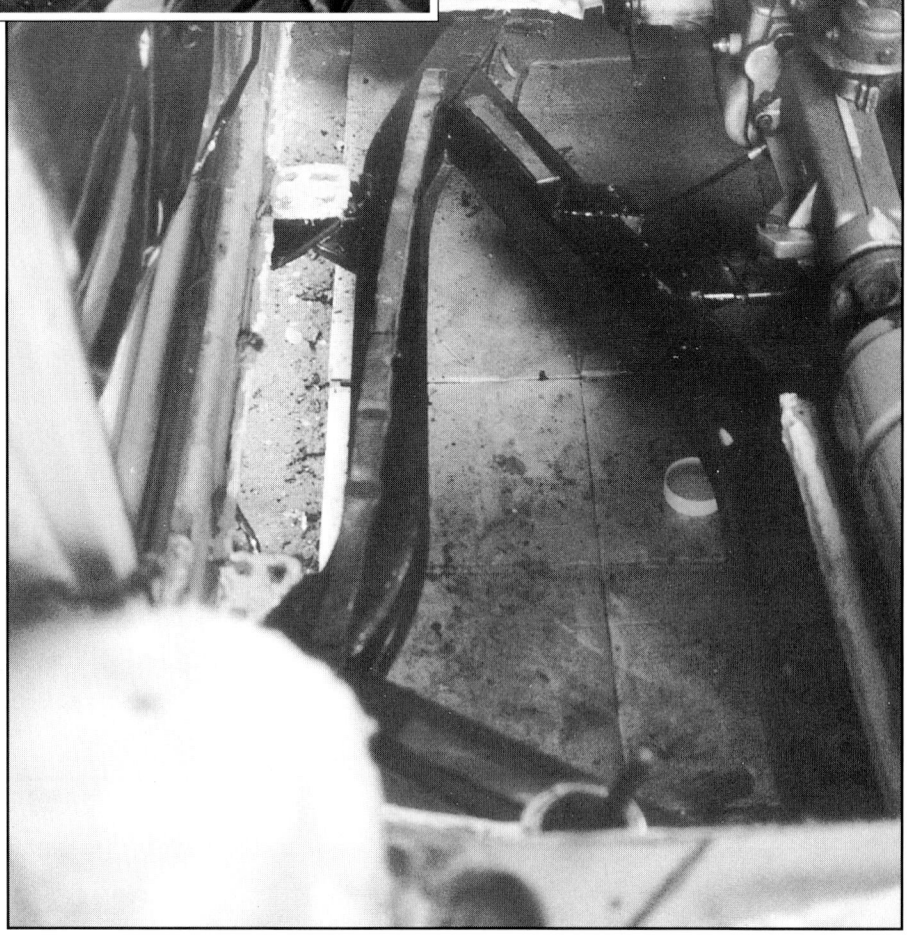

... weld the new floorpan into place and seal all joints ...

... before applying protective paint to the new panel and fixing to the chassis with new bolts and washers ...

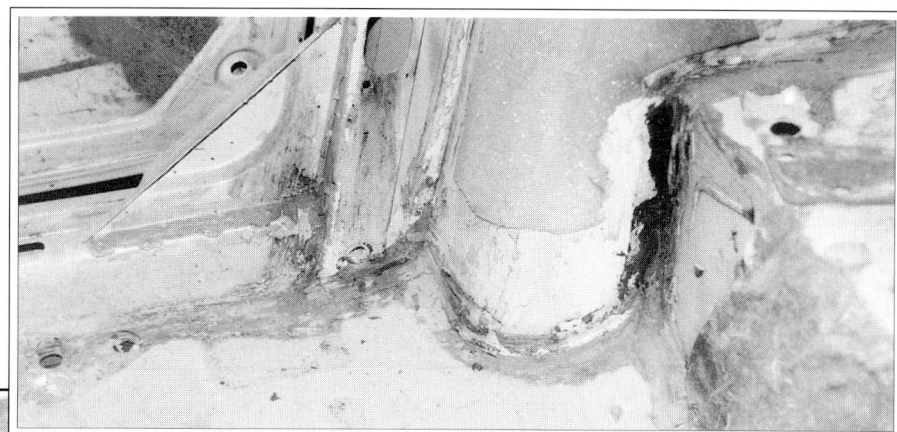

... and then repeating the procedure on the other side of the car.

This photo, taken from the transmission area of a body removed from its chassis, shows how the underside of the floor and the inner sills can rot.

Ideally, the front suspension needs lubricating every 1000 miles to inhibit wear.

The rear suspension and differential mounting points areas of the chassis need to be examined closely for signs of rust. This chassis is in fine shape!

regarded with deep suspicion. Some say that the worst affected are the American cars for some unknown reason.

Check the trailing arm mountings. Being double skinned at each end they are particularly prone to rotting at the bottom - due to sweating - and then collapsing. Examine the centre section just ahead of the trailing arm members which can also rot.

The differential mounting points corrode where the pins go through. In particular it is the front two that are most prone to this fault and not so much the back. It's not unusual to see the box section between the front pins welded up following repairs.

It is not unknown for driveshaft torque to cause the front offside pins to pull away or drop out. This results in the differential coming loose although it is unlikely to pull completely away. It does, however, lead to a loud knock when the clutch is released which is sometimes mistaken for a worn universal joint. Rectifying this problem means that the diff. has to be removed and it's possible that someone in the past has welded it to the chassis which leads to even bigger problems.

At the front the lower wishbone bracket mounting points have a tendency to rust and can ultimately tear away from the chassis, while another weak area is the rack and pinion section crossmember. The weld points in particular are prone to corrosion.

As the front suspension needs lubricating every 1000 miles to inhibit excessive wear the lower trunnions on the vertical links should be lubricated with oil (grease solidifies).

The good news in all this is that should a chassis be in a bad way, most of the sections are still available to repair it.

New chassis & body shells

You can buy a new chassis for the TR6, but some have come in for criticism for their poor quality and, generally speaking, any new chassis needs to be checked over very carefully before being worked on.

Peter Cox of TR specialists Cox & Buckles Spares, a subsidiary of Moss Europe Ltd., told me: "The one thing I would say is that we now expect a better quality chassis than was ever produced by Rubery Owen, the original suppliers, but which the general public never saw. If they had seen one as it left the factory, it would probably have put them off TRs for life!

"Peter Buckles and myself bought the last 40 or so chassis via a salvage dealer in Birmingham in the mid to late Seventies. Despite being brand new, they looked secondhand, were full of dampness inside, had a poor weld quality and were generally rusty. I've also seen examples of original chassis where they have been bent to make things fit on the assembly line. That sort of thing is less acceptable nowadays as people's standards are now so much higher."

Problems that can occur with today's new chassis, it seems, stem from the fact that there is sometimes a lack of a proper quality control in current day production. "I know three of the chassis companies reasonably well," Cox told me, "and their problem is that they usually work up to a tight deadline and in some cases the customer is taking away the chassis still hot. It means that there is very little chance of having the quality properly checked."

It is worthwhile, therefore, heeding the advice of Darryl Uprichard of Racetorations when he warns: "The offerings from some of the chassis manufacturers are shoddy and inferior and shouldn't be touched with a barge-pole. It pays to look around."

There have also been problems with the new bodyshells. Following the great success with its MGB and Midget, British Heritage was sufficiently encouraged to go ahead with one for the TR6. Unfortunately, though, it never took off in anything like the same way as the MG items; a real shame when it is realised that countless miracles had been performed in finding so many of the original tools. While it was originally finished off at Canley, the TR6 was assembled in a number of locations, such as at the Speke plant on Merseyside, and so the likelihood of finding any of the original manufacturing equipment was thought to be beyond hope. Once the sleuths started and got their noses on the scent, however, it was astonishing just what they were able to locate. On the other hand you do need a fairly large dustsheet to cover a 750 ton press!

Whether it was the scare stories over the build quality of new bodies or simply a reflection of the worldwide recession, the shells never proved to be as popular as had been anticipated.

After the initial rush to buy them in 1992, sales dwindled considerably thereafter. Even two years later, Moss was still holding something like 15 in stock. It was a situation in stark contrast to the Midget and MGB shells which have sold well from the moment they were announced. The sluggish sales, together with the amount of difficulties experienced, probably means that Heritage will, after a short batch of 25 left-hand drive shells produced in

The TR's 6-cylinder engine is a robust unit that should be rumble and rattle-free and, although the injection system is a well known problem area, it can be made reliable with relative ease.

73

Gearboxes are usually a relatively problem-free area. This one has no overdrive.
(Courtesy Gregory Cassar)

Careful and thorough restoration can result in a superb concours quality car like this CR series TR6!

late 1994, not be producing any more for the TR6 for the foreseeable future.

Engine & gearbox

When it comes to the engine, there is always a big question mark over the fuel injection system. Not only was Triumph the first large manufacturer to adopt fuel, or petrol as it was referred to at the time, injection but it was unique in using the Lucas Mark II mechanical system. Nowadays, of course, we realise that you cannot do mechanically what you can do electronically, but it was a bold first attempt.

Basically Lucas adapted a windscreen wiper motor (which perhaps says it all) that drove a gear-type mechanism. It found its way onto TR5s, most non-American TR6s and the 2.5PI saloons and estates. While it gave the Triumph range a Unique Selling Point there are a number of things that conspire against it, not least of which is that it tends to go wrong at the blink of an eye and is reputed to age the cylinder head prematurely. It is best to be aware of the problems that can be caused but on no account should you be put off from the buying the car.

Check that the engine fires up and that on a test drive there are no signs of hesitancy or poor pick up. A tip worth knowing is that if the car starts from cold without the need for the choke, then you know there are problems. Even if you are satisfied with the injection system's performance, it is very worthwhile having it serviced by a specialist as soon as you take possession of the car, unless there is documentary proof from the vendor that it has had one within the last two years or five thousand miles.

The engine itself is a lusty unit and should be rumble and rattle-free. Unless it has been seriously abused the only potential danger area is that due to the constraints imposed by a long stroke design - narrow bearings and a thin thrust washer - there is the possibility of crankshaft endfloat. A sign of a healthy engine, however, is a 60psi oil pressure at 2000rpm when warm. Blue oil smoke should be noticeable by its absence.

Despite the stresses carried by the layshaft as we have already mentioned, the gearbox is generally a fairly sound unit. Do not expect, though, the refinement of a modern box: a heavy clutch pedal is par for the course.

Overdrive is unquestionably a worthwhile option. As already mentioned, if the car is pre-1973 it will have the 'A' type Laycock de Normanville overdrive unit operating on three gearbox ratios while, from 1973 on, it will be fitted with the 'J' operating on two gearbox ratios. Overdrive problems usually stem from a dirty or faulty solenoid or faulty relay.

Unless you are buying a TR6 in premier condition with a recent rebuild history and with documentation to prove it, it is worth bearing in mind that the initial cost of the car is but the start of a continual drain on your finances. That is not to mean that you will always be shelling out money to put things right, but simply to keep the car in good fettle. If you regard her as a mistress that demands constant love and attention, even if you are not in the mood, you will be rewarded in kind for years to come.

V

LIVING WITH A TR6

So you've bought the love of your life, the car you have been yearning for as long as you can remember. You've been through the rigmarole of checking it over and it has met the criteria you set yourself. You are now at the beginning of a love affair that could last years or else you could have sown the seeds of events that will end in despair, divorce and a severe dwindling of the bank account.

As with most classic cars the TR6 gives you a variety of choices over style of ownership which broadly fall into three categories. You may be a perfectionist - some might say obsessive - about keeping it as original as possible and even enter it into concours. You love the car as much as an enthusiast less besotted with detail perfection, but show it in a different way.

Alternatively, you might be the person who wants the car for the sheer enjoyment of driving it. You do not intend to take it out on the road every day but on high days, holidays and when the sun shines. You probably won't mind too much if the car shows some signs of wear and tear.

The final category is the person who wants it to go faster. You love your TR6 but see it as a means to an end, that end being the race track. To go about fulfilling your ambition of being the racing champion of the Triumph world with a TR6 that will blow everyone else into the weeds, please refer to the next chapter.

The role of the perfectionist is the most difficult. All the details of authenticity will be known by heart when they are pertinent to your car. You will know, or will find out, whether it has the proper pattern on the seats, the right spokes on the steering wheel and is wearing the correct wheels. You will not be at all concerned that modern tyres might give better grip because it will be far more important to you that your car is wearing the correct original equipment rubber.

As the everyday enthusiast you will look at your beloved from a different viewpoint. Driving enjoyment and the satisfaction of having the car of your childhood will be the main criteria. Whilst you do not expect it to do the same things as the modern family car you drive around in every day, you do want it to start on the button, to get from A to B without any problems and you'll be most disappointed if it breaks down anywhere. You will therefore have to get to know its little foibles and be aware of the obtuse side of its nature. One of these foibles, for sure, will be the injection system.

Fuel injection system

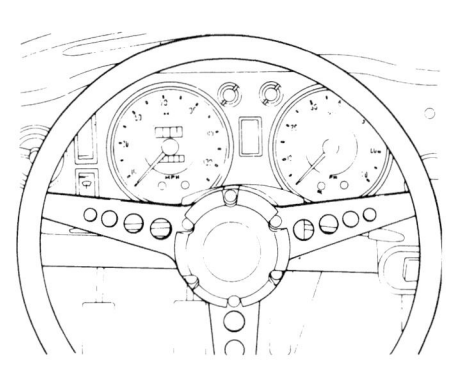

It will certainly pay you to learn as much about the fuel injection system as possible so that, should the car come to a grinding halt in the middle of nowhere, or perhaps worse, in the centre of a very busy intersection, you can diagnose the symptoms and just possibly coax the thing back into life. You will have to bear in mind, though, that while the system has been around for more than a quarter of a century and therefore all its problems and weaknesses are known, nothing can overcome the fact that it is fundamentally a poor design. It is also complicated and needs the fuel pump, pressure relief valve, metering unit and injectors working in unison under the continuous high pressure of around 106-110psi. In contrast a modern system operates at around 25-30psi. This stress sooner or later leads to unreliability, and when it does go wrong it is expensive to repair. Most of the time, though, the fault turns out to be electrical, and usually associated with poor connections.

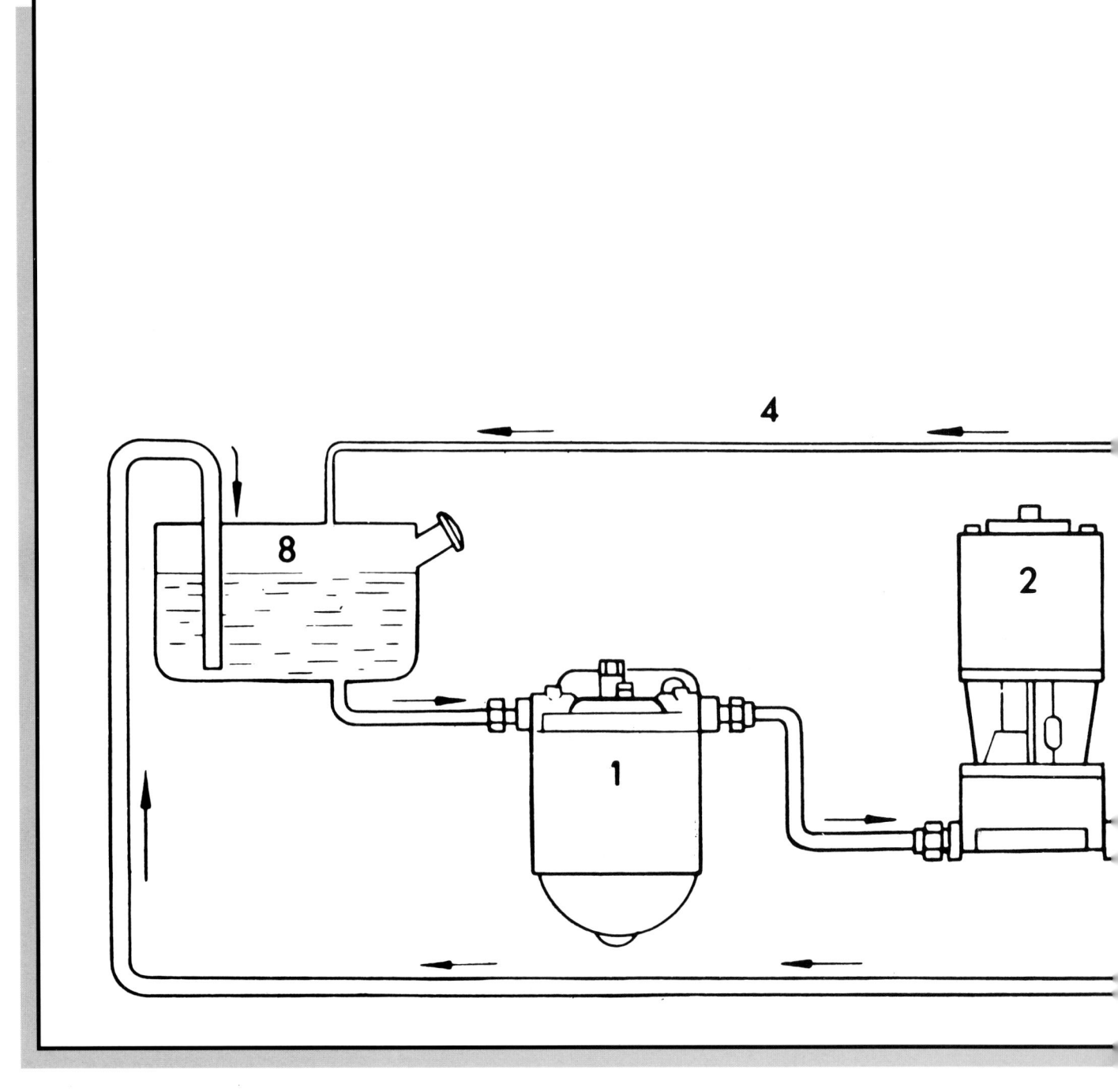

It should not be forgotten that Lucas did recommend fairly stringent service intervals for its system with a major overhaul at 35,000 miles and things needing to be done every 6000 and 12,000 miles. Your car's system should therefore have been reconditioned at least once in its life by now.

One of the unfortunate by-products of the current 'greening' of petrol is that the metering unit is robbed of

Schematic of the fuel injection system.
1. *Filter.*
2. *Pump.*
3. *Pressure relief valve.*
4. *Lubricating fuel return.*
5. *Metering distributor.*
6. *Vacuum control pipe.*
7. *Injector pipes.*
8. *Fuel tank.*

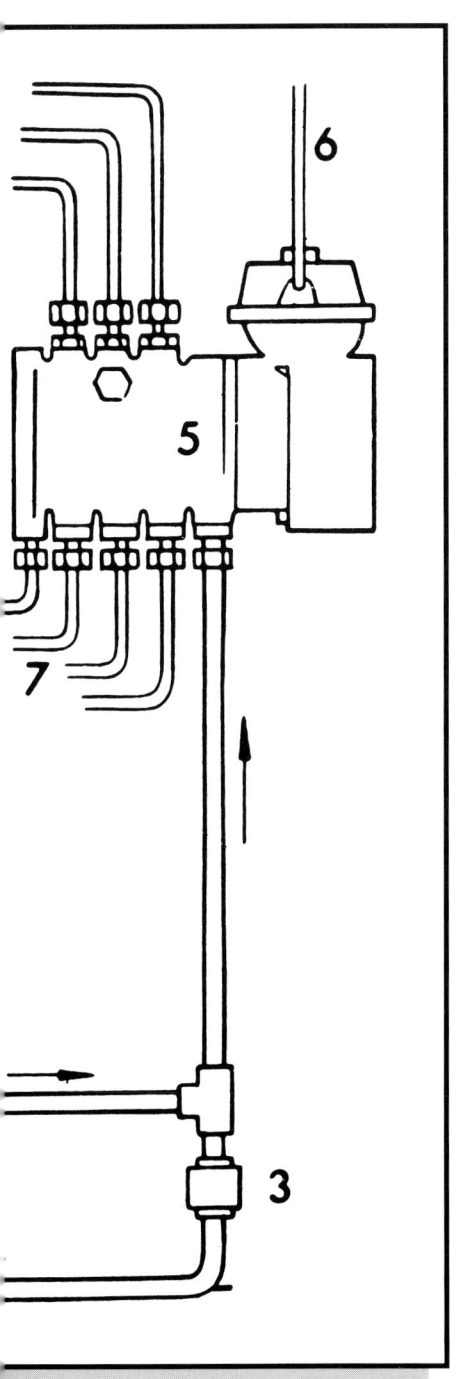

the lubrication it requires due to the decreased lead content. In particular it is an internal valve, which does not have any form of seal and relies entirely on the close machine tolerances of just millionths of an inch, which most needs the lead. Lack of lubrication leads to overheating, causing the fuel to vaporise which, in turn, causes even more overheating as the pump spins frantically without resistance. The net result is a stalled engine as the fuel flow is cut.

As is well known amongst owners, the Lucas pump is very prone to overheating on hot days. A favourite old trick is to wrap a cold, wet rag around the pump, although this is only good for temporary relief. A longer term solution is to plumb a cooling coil onto the fuel return line.

Early fuel tanks had a poorly located fuel pick-up pipe which can suck on air during left-handers causing the engine to cut out. The symptoms of this problem can be relieved by keeping the tank at least half full.

If you are not too concerned about yours being a concours car, it may even be worth considering re-routing the fuel line away from the exhaust pipe. You must ensure, though, that quarter inch steel pipe is used as alternatives may not withstand the system's 110psi operating pressure. Another option is to shroud the fuel line from the heat with asbestos foil or even polyester foam in the right places.

It is a rewarding exercise to clean out the fuel tank once a year since dirt and rust will play havoc with the filters and, if such debris blocks the outlet pipe (or poor connections in the fuel pump electrical circuit), it can lead to the engine intermittently cutting out.

The *TR Driver* published a series of articles on the fuel injection system in 1992 and 1993 and I am indebted to the club for its permission in allowing me to paraphrase them. For the full nitty gritty, though, you will need to see issues 1992 edition 3 (TR5/6 fuel injection preliminary checks), 1992 edition 5 (TR5/6 Bosch fuel pump conversion), 1992 edition 6 (TR5/6 injection fault finding), 1993 edition 3 (TR5/6 fuel pump repairs) and 1993 edition 6 (TR5/6 throttle linkages and injectors).

It must be stressed that there is a real shortage of components for the injection system because parts are no longer available from Lucas. Not even a company like Moss can offer any units from the system on an outright sale basis. Therefore, if you have any doubts about working on the system yourself, consider having the work done by a professional: finding a replacement for a component damaged through inexperience will be hard.

When misfiring occurs the first thing to do is look at the plugs since they need changing every 5000 miles. If they are not this old check that they are not fouled and that the gap is 0.025in/0.63mm. Run your eye over the distributor cap to see it is in perfect condition and that the points are at their proper 0.025in/0.63mm setting. The ignition leads should not be broken, split or burnt and the throttle butterflies must be correctly set. Check that there is a clearance of 0.004 to 0.008in (0.10 to 0.20mm) between the overfuel lever and its adjustment screw.

The static ignition timing is 11 degrees BTDC. If using a strobe it should be 20 degrees BTDC at 800rpm on early cars and 4 degrees BTDC at 800rpm on later ones. The former are identified by a vacuum advance pipe

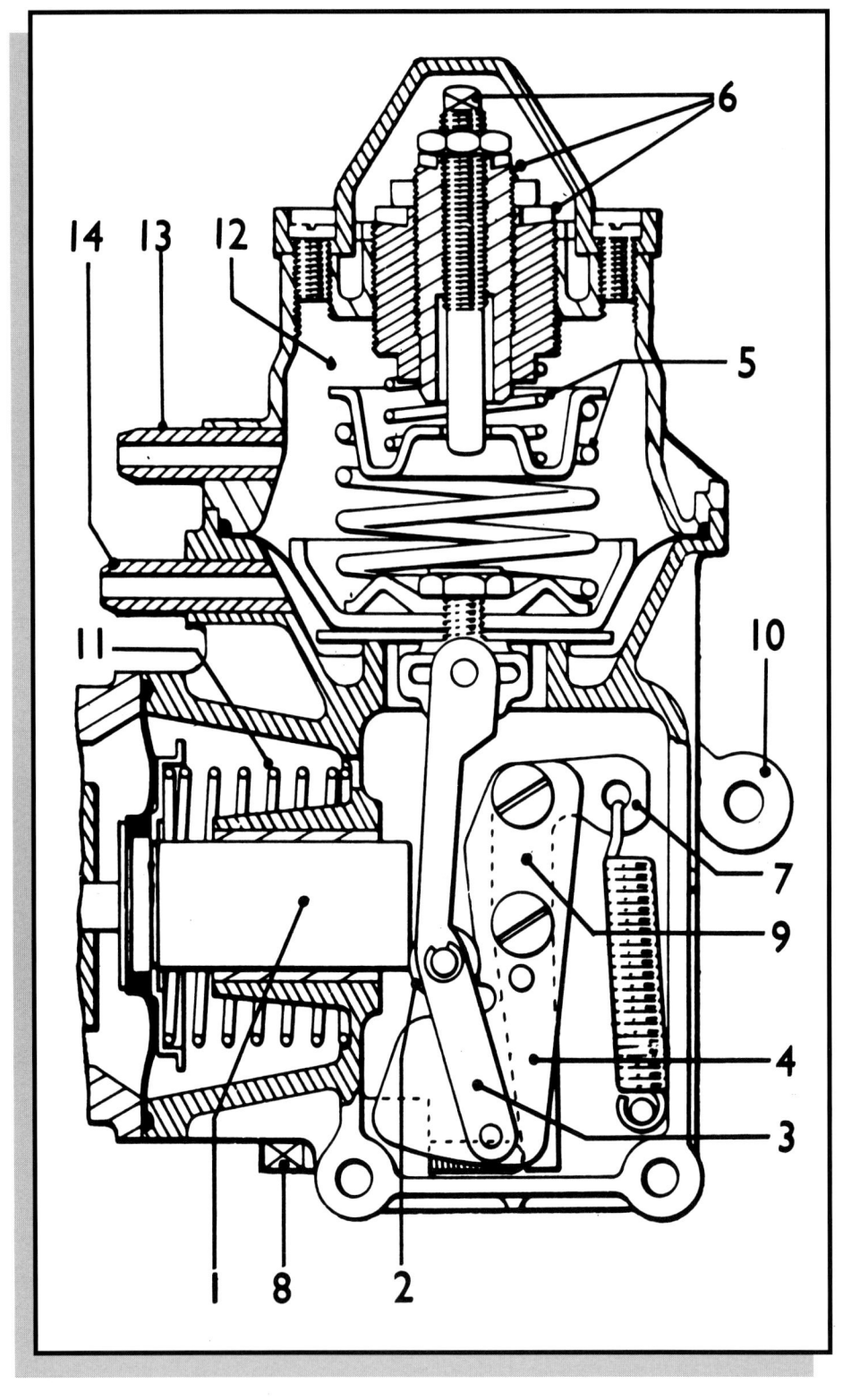

Fuel injection system control unit (attaches to metering unit).
1. Cam followers.
2. Rollers.
3. Control links.
4. Fuel cam (or datum track).
5. Calibration springs.
6. Calibration screws.
7. Fuel cam carrier.
8. Full load setting screw.
9. Carrier pivot point.
10. Excess fuel lever.
11. Balance spring.
12. Depression chamber.
13. To manifold.
14. To atmosphere.

so check the battery and charging system. If the system draws more than 5.5 amps it is indicative that there is either a mechanical problem or else there is a short circuit in the armature windings. The light grade wiring found in the fuel pump circuit in some of the early cars should be replaced by heavier 0.012in/ 0.2mm grade as used in the headlamp circuit.

If the idling is rough check the throttle butterflies are synchronised and that the fuel pipes are correctly connected to the right injectors. It is often just one cylinder that creates the problems: dirt or an air leak being the usual cause with the culprit often being number five cylinder. This cylinder is often afflicted by a poor seal on the back of the metering unit because it's tucked away where it cannot be easily reached.

Leaking connections and damaged washers on injector pipes can lead to under-fuelling, while damaged seals between the base of the outlet connection and the sleeve can cause over-fuelling. As a rough form of measurement an overdrive car should return 27mpg on a run and 20mpg in town. A car running too rich will be identified by having black soot in the tailpipe which can be confirmed by holding a white piece of card about 15 inches away from the exhaust pipe while the engine (which should be at full operat-

while a green dome atop the metering unit identifies the latter.

At least 11 volts is required to operate the injection system properly when the engine is under load and it should not draw more than 5.5 amps,

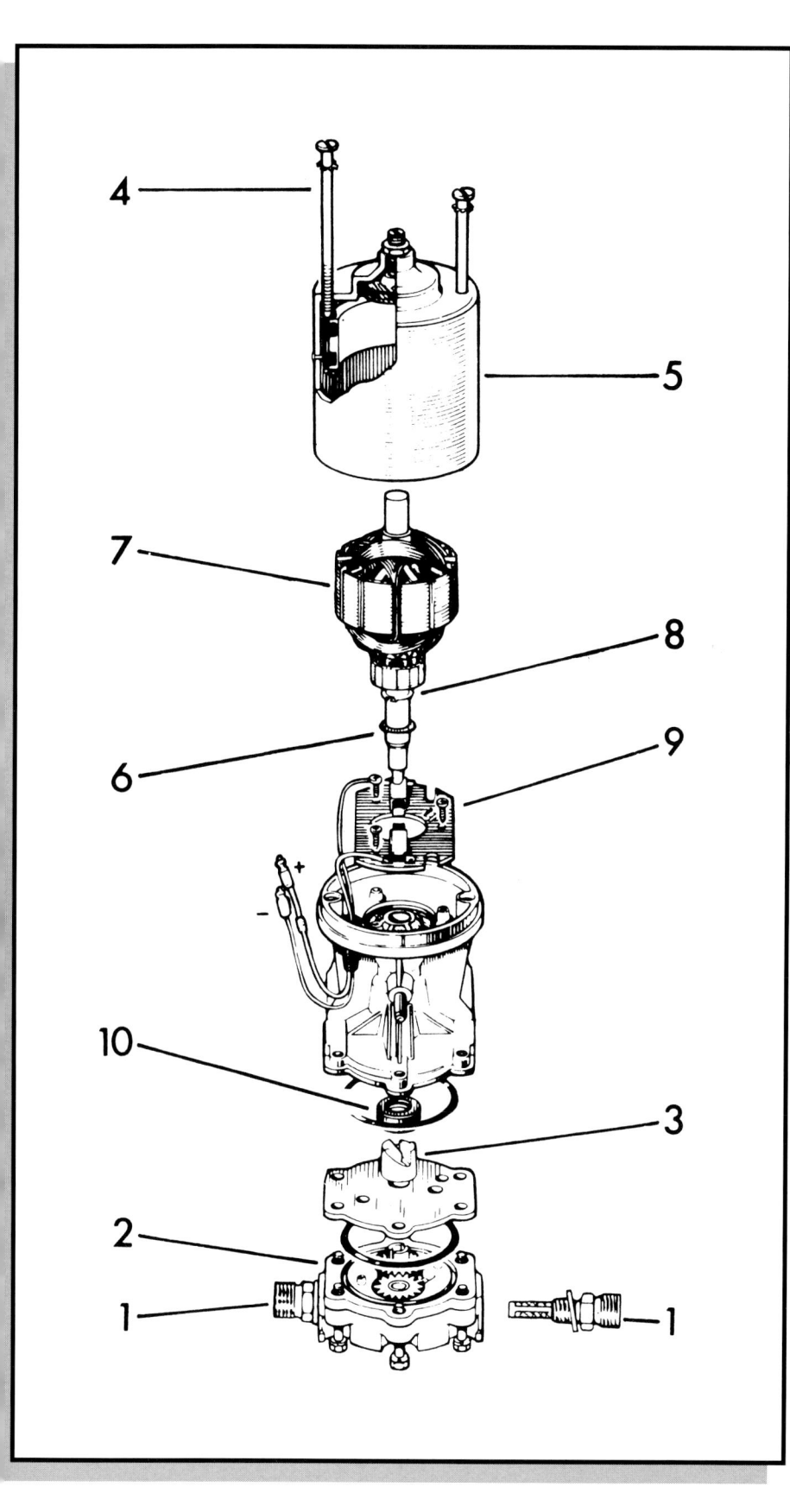

Exploded view of Lucas high pressure fuel pump.
1. Inlet union (left), outlet union and strainer (right).
2. Pump gear assembly.
3. Drive coupling.
4. Through bolt.
5. Cover and permanent magnet.
6. Thrust washer.
7. Armature.
8. Circlip.
9. Brush carrier.
10. Shaft seal.

ing temperature) is run at 1500rpm for a few minutes. If the card becomes covered in soot your suspicions will be confirmed. If too much fuel is being consumed also check for leaks in the system and check the operation of the over-fuel lever.

The injectors should be good for 30,000 miles but need to be periodically checked; however it's not a job done lightly. Following the advice printed in the *TR Driver*, lightly grip each injector pipe between thumb and finger with the pipes kept apart to avoid reflected pulses. If the pulse is weak or completely missing in the two pipes which are consecutive in the firing order, the first injector of the pair may be blocked. The consecutive pairs are 1-5, 5-3, 3-6, 6-2, 2-4, 4-1.

Switch off the engine when checking an injector, remove the clamp and withdraw it for examination. If the lower part is wet, the internal seal has probably perished and it is unserviceable, whilst one with a loose top also needs to be renewed.

The next stage is to start the car to observe the spray pattern of each injector in turn. This test must be undertaken by a professional mechanic as it would be easy to set the car or yourself on fire. The spray, which should be directed into a glass jar for safety, should be fine and clean and form a 60 degree hollow cone without any dribbling or spluttering.

If an injector is blocked a screwdriver can be used to tap the injector body (with the tip uppermost) until it starts to spray. If there is still no sign of life the spiked end should be moved gently from side to side (care must be taken not to break the spring).

Having checked, and if necessary renewed, all six injectors, the next job for the professional mechanic is to bleed the air from the injector system. With the injector clamps off, the engine should be cranked with the choke fully pulled out until fuel appears at three or four of the injectors. This should be enough to start the car and coax the others back to life. Then gently drive it a short distance without accelerating to expel all the air from the system. As soon as the engine runs evenly, replace the injector clamps.

If all the above have been checked and the car still refuses to run cleanly, it may be worthwhile adjusting the pressure relief valve. Connect a gauge that registers up to 120psi/8.5kg cm sq between the fuel line and metering unit and take a reading with the ignition on but the engine off. If it takes several seconds to show a reading, tap the pressure relief valve sharply and watch for a sudden increase on the gauge. Any response indicates a faulty valve.

If the gauge remains dead, switch off the ignition and disconnect the fuel return pipe from the pressure relief valve to reveal a nylon screw which increases the pressure by 5psi/0.3kg cm sq every quarter turn clockwise. If this does not work, there could well be a blockage in the fuel line or a faulty pump.

If the commutator in the motor is dirty or singed, rub it with a very fine emery paper until it begins to shine. If removing the magnets, slide them out very carefully to avoid damage. Bearings and bushes fail only rarely.

The pump mechanism is manufactured to very fine tolerances, the production line figure for overall clearance between the gears being between 2 and 8 thousandths of an inch. Pumps outside this tolerance will simply not allow the system to perform efficiently. Excess wear therefore indicates the need for a new pump.

When reassembling the pump replace if possible the seal between the pump and the motor. Also avoid damage to the seal at the base of the pump body. Ensure that the assembly marks on the yoke and body are aligned otherwise the rotation will be reversed. Before refitting check the end float by slackening the nut and screwing in the adjuster until you feel slight resistance. Then screw back one quarter turn. Refit the pump, ensuring all the unions are tight. Clean away excess fuel, reconnect the battery and switch the ignition on. The sound of the pump will change when the filter is filled. The engine will now start without the need to bleed the system.

One solution for an easier life is to replace the Lucas item with a Bosch fuel pump, but this needs some consideration as it is not a straightforward substitute. The German unit cannot pump fuel up from a lower level and needs a minimum flood feed of 2.6 litres per minute and preferably 5 litres per minute. If it is simply located on the boot floor to suck up fuel from the tank below, it can only manage 1 litre per minute so the answer is to fit it in a specially damped bracket to the wall of the spare wheel well.

If contemplating fitting a Bosch pump it is important to remember that while the Lucas pump draws between 3.5 and 5.5 amps, the Bosch takes 9 amps and so needs a separate feed and relay. The Bosch pump will not deliver an adequate fuel supply at 10 volts or less and, for optimum pump performance, the battery's operating voltage must not fall below 11.5 volts.

Pumfords have acquired a lot of experience in the fourteen years they have been in existence and know the Lucas system inside out. As one of Britain's leading fuel injection specialists they have developed an electronic fuel injection system which not only accepts unleaded fuel but makes the TR6 as svelte as a BMW. The engine is capable of ticking over all day while fuel consumption, even above legal road speeds, is still around 30mpg. If the mechanical Lucas system is replaced by an electronic one it makes a great deal of sense to incorporate a fuel cut-off device so that if the car is involved in a serious accident with the power still switched on, the risk of fire is reduced since fuel does not continue to be pumped through the system.

To avoid the problems of fuel injection altogether it makes a great deal more sense, according to Racetorations, to replace the whole damn caboodle with carburettors. Not the relatively

Front suspension, viewed from the front. It is essential that all bushes, bearings and balljoints are in good shape and lubrication every 1000 miles is recommended.

inefficient Strombergs but a pair of 1.75 inch SUs or triple Webers. Not only are they more user-friendly but they can also return better fuel economy figures than the original injection system if properly installed.

Such suggestions, though, are disliked by the true aficionado who argues that the cost of a triple carb set is very expensive and even when well set-up cannot match the performance of a fuel injected system. Much, of course, depends, on what the car is being used for. An SU conversion would probably be enough for the person who wants to use the car every day as it is so trouble-free and the difference in its performance and that of a fuel injected car is more in the mind than in fact.

For those who feel it necessary for whatever reason to have a 'green' car it is possible to convert the engine to accept unleaded fuel. Such a move, of course, necessitates a move away from the standard injection system although it is possible to have an appropriate conversion done at a cost . . . One figure quoted in the course of researching this book, for example, was around a third the value of a typical TR6.

The TR engine will run on unleaded fuel after the fitting of an appropriate set of valve inserts in the exhaust valve seats together with modified guides and valves. This modification, however, does carry a certain risk in that it is not unknown for such inserts to loosen. The TR which finished third on a classic Monte Carlo rally a few years ago, for example, ingested just such an insert during the event. Whilst this could have meant curtains for the engine, luck was on the crew's side for the insert was simply blown out of the exhaust, unbeknown to the driver who was only aware of a modest drop in performance. It was not until the engine was stripped down after the event that the extent of the problem was realised. An 'unleaded' cylinder head should be good for at least 50,000 miles. An original head should last at least 100,000 miles and there is every likelihood that it will do that much again.

Moving away from the engine and the injection system, there is very little that goes wrong with the car as long as

83

Front suspension, viewed from the rear. The stub axle carrying the front hub and brake disc can be prone to failure at high mileages. The lower wishbone should, frequently, be checked for cracks.

it is treated and maintained with respect for its age.

Gearbox
Gearboxes can become noisy due to wear in the front main bearing and layshaft. The Stag gearbox used from mid-1971 onwards is by far the better unit but it is still handicapped by the same poor basic design which overstresses the lay gear.

Watch out for failing synchromesh on second gear. While there are plenty of synchro rings available, they are of very variable quality. If a shoddy set is fitted not only will the rings wear out prematurely but their progressive failure will cause all sorts of other problems such as the baulk rings not working properly.

If you want to customise your car, albeit to the rage of the purist, you can reposition the overdrive switch to the gear lever as on the Triumph 2000s and Stag as well as shorten the throw.

Stub axles
Amongst the most highly stressed items in the car are the front stub axles, each of which endures severe loads and, when broken, immediately causes a wheel to fall off. Each stub axle carries a substantial proportion of the weight of the car at all times: however, when cornering one side will be carrying one and a half tons and when braking the load is substantially increased by weight transfer. While stub axles cannot be checked at the time of purchase it is well worth replacing them unless you have documentary proof stating the date they were bought and the mileage they have since clocked up. It is recommended that stub axles are renewed after 60,000 miles of use.

Brakes
As long as it is in good working order the standard brake set-up is perfectly adequate for the task, especially if Aeroquip hoses are used. The fitting of these high quality hoses ensures that the brake pedal action is 'hardened' up. The servo found on the later cars also needs to be in good condition.

If the brake hydraulic system needs to be bled, always start at the bleed valve furthest from the master cylinder. On right-hand-drive cars, start at the nearside rear, then offside rear, nearside front and finish at the offside front. Use a mirror image procedure for left-hookers. Top up the master cylinder frequently during the bleeding operation, otherwise air will enter the system.

Suspension
The suspension and steering are often the cause of poor handling: an accumulation of wear and/or softening with age in individual bushes and ball joints can take the edge off handling and even make the car dangerous. It's recommended that bushes and ball joints be renewed whenever they show the slightest signs of wear or fatigue.

Stiffened and lowered springs at the front are rather wasted on a road car and little needs to be done at the back other than keeping everything in first class order.

Each time you take off your car's front wheels, check the lower wishbone mountings for signs of cracking. If this check is neglected there is the possibility that one day a wishbone will tear away from the chassis with ruinous results.

Seat belts
The seat belt mounting points are vital safety areas so, if your prime concern is not originality, it's recommended that they be modified. Instead of having the mountings simply bolted onto the floorpan in the standard fashion, it's worthwhile to enlarge the mounting points on the chassis and weld large steel plates behind to help spread the load in the event of a collision.

New body shells
At some stage you may decide that the day has come for a ground-up rebuild. If this is your intention there are a number of specialists who can provide advice and every imaginable part.

If you are going the whole hog and using a Heritage shell as the basis of a rebuild, do not expect sweetness and light all the way. In my research for this book, I interviewed a well known stalwart of the TR6 brigade who vowed never to use one again. In a litany of woe he found that the gap between the sills and the doors was unacceptably large, the bonnet locating pins were one and a half inches out, the boot lid was out of alignment and the petrol tank, which normally takes about half an hour to fit, took him four hours as all the locating holes had to be elongated. Another bugbear included fitting the hood as the three holes on the B post did not line up, nor did he like the fact that there was rather an uneven coat of latex underneath which had been rather clumsily applied. However, when it comes to panel fit and finish, it has to be remembered that the TR6 was never a conventional mass production car in the way that the MGB or Midget were with their monocoque bodyshells.

"I think most people expected to get a new car less wheels and an engine," Peter Cox, who is heavily involved in marketing the Triumph bodyshells through Moss Europe, explained to me, "but Heritage knew they couldn't do that. The shells have been going to inexperienced hands, often in less than ideal working conditions, where they have been built and painted prior to any potential problems having been sorted out." The results in some cases, according to Darryl Uprichard of Racetorations, have proved to be "a real dog's dinner."

The difficulties inherent in using a new shell have been compounded when rebuilders tried to fit them onto one of the poorly manufactured new chassis and found that nothing lined up. First they drilled holes in what they thought were the right places in the chassis and then, finding the holes did not match those in the bodyshell, drilled yet more holes in the bodyshell to try to rectify the mismatch. One thing that should be borne in mind, however, is that because the bodies and chassis of standard production cars were originally bolted together by hand by skilled workers, there was a latitude of up to a quarter of an inch with many of the holes slotted/enlarged and packing pieces judiciously used during the original build process. While it was of no relevance to the customer of the time, it's a different matter when it comes to a rebuild.

While the Heritage shell has had its fair share of criticism, Peter Cox is rather dismissive of that coming from the trade: "We're selling the Heritage shell for roughly £2500 and for them [specialist traders] to produce even an equivalent one would cost a minimum of twice that amount and, more realistically, £6000-£8000. If you take £2500 off £6000 you can do an awful lot with £3500 if you're a trader. I think one or two of the better specialists have responded to this. They may have spent £1000 worth of labour on the shell but then have ended up with a brand new one for £3,00. That is still only half the cost of a rebuild."

What has been a particular drawback, though, is that every one of the 100 shells produced has been different. "This has caused us more problems than ever," Peter Cox told me, "because we just don't know what to look for. What might be wrong with one is perfectly alright on another." To try to put matters right Moss found it necessary to produce its own checklist. To put matters into perspective, though, I was told that of the 85 shells that had been sold by the autumn of 1994, there had been problems with 20 of them of which just 5 caused major headaches and actually cost money to put right.

What did not help, it seems, was that in the middle of their production run there was a change in the paint supplier. While the colour remained the same off-white, there was quite a variation in the paint quality, although it has been impossible to ascertain whether it was the older or later cars that were affected.

When rebuilding the TR6, according to the experts, it is vital to have a bare metal dummy run and bolt the shell down onto the chassis. Preferably the chassis should be on its wheels and the engine and gearbox in place as well as the doors, boot, bonnet and even the windscreen. This is to ensure that the chassis is flexed to its normal position and everything lines up exactly as it will on the final rebuild, particularly shutlines and gaps which need to be as perfect as possible. Once this has been done and all fit problems resolved the car can be dismantled for spraying prior to the real rebuild.

Even if you do not want to take the complete rebuild route, a well maintained TR6, even a fuel injected one, will last for years. They're fun to drive, are of the bulldog breed of car no longer made and rarely seen on the road and, let's face it, not really PC (politically correct) for the millennium. They should therefore be loved and cherished and, above all, used.

Over 20 years with a TR6

David Wright bought his TR6 new in 1970 for £1430. The Signal Red car has since done some 90,000 miles and, despite rear end damage some years ago, has retained its original paintwork except for the rear panel which is now painted body colour. Originally these panels were painted matt black on production cars but, having mistakenly painted it red, David decided that it looked just as good in that colour so he left it as it was. Being lanky prompted David to fit a smaller steering wheel to make things easier in the driving seat.

When new, there was continuing trouble with the Lucas fuel injection system on this car which the garage/supplier could not put right. Eventually David obtained the special meter to measure line pressure and injector settings, and has since carried out all tests, adjustments and repairs himself. Armed with the correct workshop manual, the right tools and some patience, these jobs can be carried out by owners who have appropriate mechanical skills. David has fitted a canister-type oil filter to replace the original renewable element arrangement. He did not go for the optional overdrive, but later fitted high-lift cams and a stage two head which now gives the car a top speed in the high 120s.

David admits that his ownership of this TR6 has been entirely undramatic as nothing serious has ever gone wrong with it. Layshaft bearing wear in the four-speed gearbox was easily remedied by fitting a reconditioned gearbox - surprisingly, it was cheaper to do this than repair the existing 'box. The fuel pump has overheated on occasion, especially once during that hot British summer of 1976, but a later modification using fuel to cool the body of the Lucas pump has been successful.

Driving back from a photo location, David opened up the throttle and the TR6 shot away, making that noise I always remembered from my youth. The rear end squats down as the power is turned on, but the speed mounts up surprisingly quickly. 0-60 can come up in as little as 8.2 seconds - very quick even by today's standards.

It's a car that still turns heads today, it's uncompromising macho looks making it stand out from the blandness of today's' econoboxes. If one discounts the TR7, which had nothing whatever in common with any other TR, then the TR6 made a fitting end to the TR range, allowing the model to bow out on a high note.

When they were new

An interesting contemporary report on living with a new TR6 comes from *Motor Sport* Deputy Editor Clive Richardson. He was given a TR6 as a company car with which he developed a love-hate relationship. Related in the November 1973 and December 1974 editions of the magazine, Richardson's words provide an insight into the trials and tribulations of running a TR6.

"When I ordered a new TR6 in Autumn last year," he starts in the November issue, "I was looked at askance by colleagues and associates. 'What on earth do you want one of those lorries for?' 'Something out of the Ark.' 'Terrible handling . . .' and all that sort of rubbish with which people without experience of them usually condemn TR6s. Certainly they are old fashioned in design and one can't compare the handling of them with, say, a Lotus Europa. But they have many attributes, including a big, beefy engine, a solid chassis and, above all, character. They're cars which have to be driven and tamed, one of the few remaining, traditional, hairy-chested sports cars. One has to know all its big or little vices before driving it on the limit. Above all, though I wanted an open sports car, it was to replace a Janspeed-modified MGB roadster and join a hopefully temporarily dormant XK150 fhc. The open sports car market is severely restricted, particularly in the middle price bracket, under £2000, restricted virtually to the TR6, Jensen-Healey and the Morgan Plus 8. The Morgan I dismissed, probably inaccurately, as being insufficiently practical, but most of all because delivery time was reputed to be counted in years, the Jensen-Healey partly because I find it unattractive - an overgrown Spitfire - and secondly because the reliability reputation of the early models amongst the members of the motoring Press was not very encouraging.

"Now what better car could I choose from the point of view of reliability than one which was moving into its 21st year of production? . . . All those years to iron out the bugs and make the TR foolproof? Or so one would think. In fact when PGN 769L ('*Pig-in-'ell*' as dubbed by his wife) was delivered to Standard House with 24 miles on the clock on February 28th this year, four months after the order was placed with

Henlys Ltd., Berkeley Square, it contained so many faults that it might well have been the first car off the line of a new model. Its general finish was appalling, mechanically it was dreadful, and it was to be another 5500 miles before this Lucas fuel-injected motor car was to run consistently on six cylinders."

The litany of woe continues. "Space precludes a full list of the faults which were present when my Mimosa yellow TR6 was delivered," Richardson complained, "so the following are just a few examples. The engine misfired below 1500rpm; the high pressure fuel pump would have drowned the noise of Concorde; the throttle had an inch of dead movement and full throttle was unavailable; the fan belt had four inches of slackness; fuel or brake pipes rattled against the bulkhead; the front pads squeaked permanently when the brakes were not applied; the driver's door fouled the wing; the wiper motor floated loose because the packing surround within its horseshoe bracket had been omitted; the heater blower wouldn't switch off and only one speed worked; the bulb had failed in the nearside repeater flasher; wind noise was terrible because the door windows were incorrectly set; paint was spilt on the carpet; paint around the door areas appeared to have been applied with a tar brush; gooey black sealer oozed out from the tail-lamp surrounds, windscreen, and hardtop windows. Oh, and then there was the rust. Rust speckles covered the headlining in the steel hardtop and the bottom rear interior corners of it were full of rust and muck; the airflow grilles, hardtop attachment nuts and facia screws were all rusty; there were several rust speckles on the hardtop and bodywork; and engine components were so rusty it looked as though it had stood in the rain for a week. As for the handling . . . . the dampers were weak and the car geometry steered even in a straight line, while all four wheels and possibly the propshaft were out of balance."

Despite all this Richardson decided to take it abroad soon after delivery. "I should have known better than to risk taking this very secondhand new car on the Continent. A mere 40 miles along the Belgian autoroute on the way down to Cologne at night the straight-six became an in-line four when the electrodes burnt away on two plugs. One of the little yellow Renault 4 rescue vehicles provided two old plugs at a price, which regained one cylinder. Ten five-cylinder miles later I found out that this TR6's claimed 11.75 gallons fuel tank exhausted itself at nine gallons, as it still does, and had to be rescued once more, another expensive experience. In Cologne I checked the injectors to find them spraying fuel and fitted a new set of plugs - but still only five cylinders, so I assumed a valve to be burnt out. Risking more serious damage - by now I was past caring - I drove the misfiring, ill-handling heap back to England and the Triumph factory."

There followed an intensive spell when the car spent most of its life at the factory during which time it was so played around with that it was about as original as that well known hammer which has had several new handles and quite a number of new heads.

Once it was sorted, though, Richardson began to enjoy the car. "Handling is very much a matter of opinion," he wrote, "very vintage and reasonably entertaining. Certainly it is nowhere near as bad as those who have never driven TR6s try to make out! It errs very much on the side of the safe understeer, for Spen King decided to fit a thicker front anti-roll bar than the TR5 had, and surprisingly high cross-country averages can be maintained. Having driven TRs on both the SP Sports and XASs, I must say I prefer the handling with SPs; the XASs hold the road much better, but they do tend to promote understeer, whereas the SPs allow the car to be thrown around quite aggressively to negate the understeer. Ultimately the XAS may be the faster tyre, but the SPs are more enjoyable. Ride, too, is vintage but only really bad bumps cause any severe discomfort. One must also learn to live with scuttle shake: after a big Healey and the XK150 I hardly notice the TR's any longer. It is much more prominent when the car is in soft-top form (this was fitted at the first visit to the factory, the car having been delivered in hardtop form), the rigid steel hardtop creating a much tauter unit."

By the end of the first report, Richardson has begun to have a grudging respect for the car, his initial disappointment at the appalling pre-delivery inspection fading with time. His follow-up report just over a year later, though, found that the old wounds had been re-opened.

"The week after the first Tale went to press the gearlever, in neutral, spun round uselessly in my hand when I tried to make a three-point turn to escape from a Hyde Park Corner traffic jam. As I was broadside across the road at the time I was not amused . . . The lever suddenly popped back into place whilst I was trying to remove the centre console after the car had been pushed across the road."

He reports on what a 15,000 mile service threw up when taken to a specialist Triumph centre. "Apart from the routine servicing, most of their time was spent putting things right which had either been done wrongly or not at all at British Leyland, Western Avenue. Bear in mind that only 3000 very gentle miles during the 50mph restriction *[a British government inspired piece of lunacy which put a blanket 50mph speed limit on all roads, including motorways, in response to threatened oil supplies during the Arab-Israeli war of 1973]* had been covered since the last Western Avenue service. Inlet and exhaust tappet settings for this engine should be 10 thou; they checked out as four exhausts set at 8 thou, the other two at 13 thou and all inlets at 6 thou. The timing was well out, having been set from the wrong mark on the front pulley; the nearside driveshaft splines were dry of grease; the propshaft had not been greased; the gearbox had been overfilled; the inner upper steering shaft had been wrongly positioned; and both rear brake adjusters were loose. Additionally a new condenser was needed and a choke cam was seizing up, minor routine failures.

Jarman *[the proprietor of the specialist company]* also spotted cracks in the tyres, including the spare and heard a worrying engine noise, which we think is excessive crankshaft end float, a common problem according to readers, and unlikely to help the engine's longevity. He also removed the rubber block in the choke slide on the metering unit, which is meant to be retained merely during the running-in period to prevent the engine being over-enriched."

This proper servicing at long last seemed to do the trick, for as Richardson reported: "The car seemed to revel in the effects of the first decent service it had received and complete with a sumpful of Duckham's oil for the first time and new Champion plugs, 'Pig-in-'ell' at last felt like a new car. To achieve this had taken 15,000 miles and goodness knows how many hours of British Leyland work before The TR Centre finally sorted out the troubles in just one day."

Apart from the replacement of a gearbox, already alluded to in an earlier chapter, the car at long last began to reward Richardson with reliability and pleasant motoring. In this catalogue of disasters, though, the one thing that did not give any trouble after initial problems, against all the odds, was the fuel injection system.

"If readers wonder why I have not yet mentioned the notorious Lucas fuel injection system which gave so much trouble in the early life of this TR6 and those of many readers, there is a good reason: astonishingly the system has not once given trouble since it was rebuilt by the Triumph Engineering Division 16,000 miles ago. Specific instructions not to touch the system have been given by me every time the rest of the car has been serviced since then, yet not a beat has been missed and the only indirect complaint has been a leaking oil seal between the metering unit and the block, replaced at the last service. Such exceptional reliability - even a single carburettor would have required more attention - I suspect lies in very careful selection of a metering unit by Triumph Engineering, because my experience certainly seems against the law of readers' averages. If every Lucas system worked as well as mine does now, doubtless we should all be praising the design to high heaven instead of damning it because of what would seem to be inconsistent engineering quality."

Despite the good manners, Richardson was still reluctant to take the car too far. "Although 'Pig-in-'ell' seems to have become relatively reliable in the last 5000 miles (touch wood), I remain too sceptical to take her too far afield, certainly on the Continent." Rather in the manner of a punch-drunk boxer, Richardson finishes the report kindly, having developed a soft spot for the car. "In spite of everything, and possibly because the infrequency of driving this car makes it more of a novelty when I do so, and again because I have a certain feeling of sympathy for her because of my critical *Motor Sport* story, I have developed a soft spot for 'Pig-in-'ell'. She has become quite one of the family and, because of inflation, may have to remain so for a long time to come: when this car was purchased in February 1973 the basic price of the hardtop model was £1387 plus £290 Purchase Tax, with another £73, including PT, asked for overdrive and £48 for a soft-top (not including tonneau), making a total of £1798; the basic price for a hardtop model today, remembering that overdrive and tonneau are now included as standard, is £1911, while a soft-top now costs £63, so my car today would cost a grand total of £2309. Nevertheless, if one could rely on better quality control and a higher standard of exterior finish, the TR6 would be good value for money if a relatively powerful two-seater, open sports car meets your needs; after all it is one of the few remaining examples of a dying breed of car . . ."

VI

SO, YOU WANT TO BE A RACER?

To want to race a TR6 will mean that you are a little bit special. Good as TR6s are, they will never beat a state of the art TR4 or the later TR7s and TR8s, so you have to accept that in taking one to the track you will be giving yourself a handicap. But before going into the nuts and bolts of what you can do and letting fly with a wad of money, it's worthwhile looking back to the time when they flew the flag for Triumph in the hands of such luminaries as Bob Tullius, Jim Dittemore, John McComb and none other than Paul Newman, not as a makeweight but in a starring role.

It was the advent of the six cylinder model that sparked it all off. The Triumph management in Britain had been quite content with the successes chalked up by the different four cylinder cars over the years. Various Le Mans expeditions from the mid-Fifties to the early Sixties and rallying escapades with TR3s, 3As and 4s had kept the marque to the fore in the public's minds while, in America, TRs had a long and distinguished history in the Sports Car Club of America's championship. The advent of the six cylinder car, though, changed things. It was time to draw a veil over sporting activities as far as Canley was concerned. However, it was just the reverse as far as the Americans were concerned for they were now being presented with an engine that had the prospect of opening up new horizons.

Kastner's TR 250K

It is more than likely that the home country would have had its way and the new six cylinder TR would have been relegated to club racing were it not for the persuasive powers of their American west coast competitions manager.

R. W. "Kas" Kastner was one of those dynamic individuals who would not take "no" for an answer. He was totally dissatisfied with the meagre competition budget which would only enable him on the west coast, and Group 44 on the east coast, to go production racing: a style of racing where the cars that raced on Sunday could be driven to work on Monday. Kastner's aspirations were far more wide ranging as he believed that Triumph had, on its hands, a machine that could really set the track alight: he pressed for more money. Undaunted by the singular lack of enthusiasm from the parent company, Kastner argued fiercely about the merits of utilising the lusty new engine in a special-bodied TR 250 to go racing in a serious way. Maintaining that, if nothing else, such a car would attract a great deal of publicity and was bound to be featured in magazines, he finally managed to unlock the funds to produce a one-off machine - not from the competition purse but from the advertising budget.

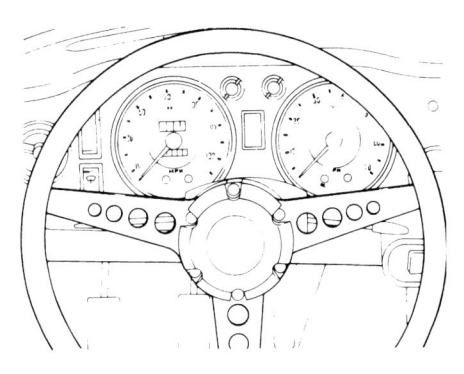

Using a hand-formed aerodynamic body designed by Pete Brock, the stylist responsible for Ford's 1965 Cobra Daytona, and made out of aluminium the TR 250K ("K" for Kastner) had its baptism of fire at the 1968 Sebring 12-hour race. And what a debut! Driven by Group 44's Bob Tullius and Jim Dittemore this 155mph machine led the first three hours of the event. Unfortunately, though, any thoughts of a fairytale debut turned to dust when it became sidelined with a broken wheel.

There was one consolation, however, which justified the project having been financed out of the advertising budget. The TR 250K got onto the front cover of the April 1968 issue of *Car and Driver* magazine. Unfortunately, in view of the impact it made, the car was then mothballed and was not seen again in competition as a works car. The work carried out on it, however, was not wasted as the lessons learnt formed the basis of the six cylinder TR's competition career.

Naturally the TR 250K's 2498cc engine was blueprinted and balanced and, with the aid of three Weber 45 DCOE carburettors, optimised valve

TR6s did well in the American sports car races once the SCCA accepted fuel injection.

dling. This in turn led to the seating position being pushed further back and the cockpit being slightly enlarged while an integral roll bar increased the car's structural integrity. The suspension was mildly tuned, even by today's standards, with front Koni shock absorbers and adjustable anti-roll bars being the only non-standard parts. The brakes were uprated with twelve inch discs and Hurst/Airheart calipers fitted all-round while the car rode on Firestone-shod 6.75 inch gold Lotus wheels.

Racing in America

Despite the involvement of Bob Tullius and Group 44, who were to go onto greater things in the 1980s with the racing XJR Jaguars, the competition TR250s, or rather TR5s as they were in fact fuel injected, were not quite able to match the best Porsche 911s and were just about on par with a Datsun SRL311 2000 Roadster driven by Bob Sharp. In that year's national run-offs, to which the top three finishers in each competition class from each of the geographical divisions were invited, Tullius and Jim Dittemore in their TR 250s had to give second best to the Porsches of Alan Johnson and Milt Minter.

The following year saw the arrival of the TR6s, in fact the same cars underneath and simply re-skinned. With the Datsuns consigned to the D-Production class it was a straight fight between Triumph and Porsche. While there was some success in claiming Division spoils, the German machines

timing, 11.6:1 compression and an exhaust header it developed in excess of 200bhp. It was redlined at 7000rpm.

According to the brief, the TR250K had to use as many standard items as possible which not only included the overdrive gearbox, rear axle and the drive shafts but also the indicators and repeaters. The chassis was stiffened with the addition of a welded tube sub-frame which also supported the engine that had been moved nine inches to the rear in the interests of weight distribution and resultant better han-

93

were never troubled by the British sports cars when it came to the final run-offs.

1970, though, was the year that not only saw the arrival of the Porsche 914/6 but, with the advent of the epochal Datsun 240Z, the applecart really was upset. While Tullius won the Northeast Division and Lee Mueller the Northern Pacific Division in TR6s, it all came to nought in the Finals. Despite setting competitive practice times Mueller eliminated himself in the warm up while Tullius, now as the sole Triumph representative, had to retire from the lead with a burnt clutch after just seven laps. The result was an astounding 1-2-3 for Datsun.

While TR6s continued to make the Finals for the next three years and were always in with a chance of victory, it was the 240Z that ultimately ruled the roost and, when the baton was passed to the 260Z the following year, it continued Datsun's successful ways.

With the arrival of the 2.8-litre fuel injected 280Z for the model year 1975, it was realised by all concerned that the TR6 days were well and truly numbered in the C-Production class. As a result it was reclassified into the D-Production class, shorn of its fuel injection, and had to have a minimum weight of 2136lbs. Its rivals now included the Jensen-Healey and the Datsun Roadster. By this time, though, it had become the tired old soldier and had to take second place to British Leyland's 'Great White Hope', the TR7.

The fact that the six cylinder car was now on the corporate backburner did not stop Group 44 entering John McComb in a race in the Northeast Division while Jim Ray and Dennis Day raced in the Southwest and Central Divisions respectively. Despite strong opposition from Datsun Roadsters, both McComb and Ray won their respective Divisions to earn places in the Finals.

It was Lee Mueller in the Jensen, though, who provided the stiffest resistance in the vital race. Starting from pole McComb was looking good when he pulled out a three second a lap lead over the Jensen driver. On lap 13, however, his times began to go awry and Mueller began to reel him in. It transpired that the TR6 had picked up slow punctures on the left front and right rear tyres but, while the tyres were slowly deflating, it still seemed that he might be able to survive to the end of the race without a pit stop.

As both cars started on their final lap it seemed that after years of trying Triumph and Group 44 were going to have the taste of the winner's champagne denied yet again. McComb dug deep into his resources, juggled the need to preserve the tyres as much as possible with the necessity of keeping Mueller at bay to take the chequered flag a mere 2.2 seconds ahead. Triumph had finally won the National Championship.

Actually it was all rather embarrassing for the company as the TR7 was now on the market. The car that "was out to steal the American road," as the adverts of the time stated, was now rather put into the shade by its predecessor which was still on sale. And, if that was not bad enough, it repeated the feat again the following year, putting even more egg on the TR7's face.

Despite McComb's success in the 1975 championship, marketing requirements dictated that Group 44 turn all its attention to the TR7. The championship-winning TR6 was therefore put up for sale at $15,000 and ended up in the hands of film star Paul Newman. The actor's enthusiasm for motor racing is well known through his involvement with the Newman-Haas team and the world publicity of running Nigel Mansell in 1993 and 1994, and Newman himself is a creditable driver. Despite not being able to compete in the Northeast Division's races with the ex-McComb car until July of 1976, Newman still did enough to qualify for the Finals at Road Atlanta.

Yet again it was Lee Mueller who turned out to be the challenger for the Championship, but this time behind the wheel of a TR7. It was Newman, though, who rather shocked everybody by claiming pole in his TR6 with a stunning 93mph lap. At the drop of the flag, though, he saw his hard earned advantage slip away when Jim Fitzgerald in a Datsun shot away into the lead followed by Mueller's TR7 and a rather aged Yenko Corvair Stinger.

As the race unfolded the Corvair fell off the track while the Datsun began to lose power and was soon dropping down the field to leave it a straight contest between "TR past versus TR future." Although Mueller had the advantage of being in front, Newman refused to give up. Slower through the corners he might be, but his TR6 had

The Cox & Buckles TR Register Championship is a favourite series for those wishing to race their TR6s. The principal behind the regulations and various classes is to give the participants an equal chance of success, whilst at the same time ensuring competitive racing.

the legs of the TR7 on the straights.

It was the final corner, though, that was the clincher: the actor made one last desperate lunge and, to the astonishment of all, came out ahead to sprint across the line by less than a nose. For the second consecutive year a TR6 had won the National Championship and with a high profile name at the wheel to boot. In normal circumstances it would have been a moment of great rejoicing for BL, but, under the circumstances, it was a case of sooner forgotten the better.

Racing in Britain

Back in the TR's home country, meanwhile, racing activities were strictly confined to amateurs and club racers. While this was of great interest to the participants, it was hardly of major concern to the outside world.

Since then TR6s have always been seen on the track, thanks to a variety of championships. Chief amongst these is the Cox & Buckles sponsored championship organised by the TR Register which has been in existence since 1984. Aimed specifically at encouraging the TR driver who would like to go motor racing, the regulations have been formulated to give every car and driver in each class an equal chance of success, at the same time ensuring close and competitive racing between the various models.

Tuning the TR6

There are a variety of ways you can take your TR6 motor racing. You may decide to go for the class where the least modification is allowed, or go to extremes and opt for one where the cars are transformed out of all recognition. In this case, though, it will be more than likely that you will require the services of a specialist company and a fair-sized budget to survive the season.

Whatever form of motor sport you decide to enter there are certain modifications you are forced to undertake if you are to take you car onto the track. A roll-over bar, for example, is *de rigueur* for even the mildest form of racing and so you will have to reconcile yourself to the fact that you will be butchering your car to some degree. You also have to bear in mind that if you wish to take your TR6 for even the occasional hillclimb or sprint where you are likely to take the needle of the rev counter

The C & B Championship Class D cars can be slightly modified but there are limitations placed upon what can be done to the engine, body, suspension and so on. This is Bob Payne ... (Courtesy Richard Dempster)

... Mark Davenport ... (Courtesy Richard Dempster)

COLOUR GALLERY

Original press release photo of an early right-hand drive TR6. (Courtesy B.M.I.H.T.)

Below & overleaf, top: HUD 638L was added to Triumph's press fleet early in 1973. It had detail changes over earlier models such as the front 'bib' spoiler, satin-finish hub trims, chrome-plated wheel nuts and centre badges, matt black wiper arms and blades, plus thicker beading on the sill edges. (Courtesy B.M.I.H.T.)

COLOUR GALLERY

COLOUR GALLERY

A beautiful CP series car which has undergone a recent restoration.

While the slight gloss applied to the dashboard of this restored car undoubtedly looks good, the original finish was matt.

Left: A comparison between a car with standard bumpers and one with the bumperettes that were fitted to late model cars destined for the US market.

99

COLOUR GALLERY

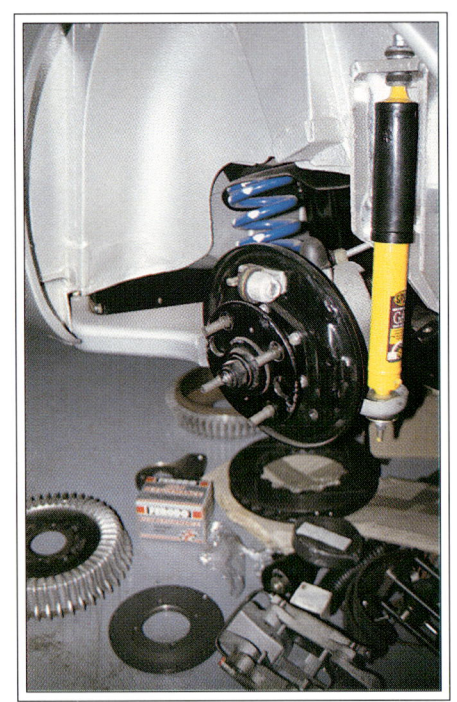

Left & below: To keep the car honest on the race track the suspension needs to be considerably stiffened with harder springs, all round Spax dampers and composite or very hard rubber bushes.

100

COLOUR GALLERY

Left: Had enough of fuel injection problems? TR specialists Racetorations advocate converting the engine to run on twin SU carburettors, as shown here.

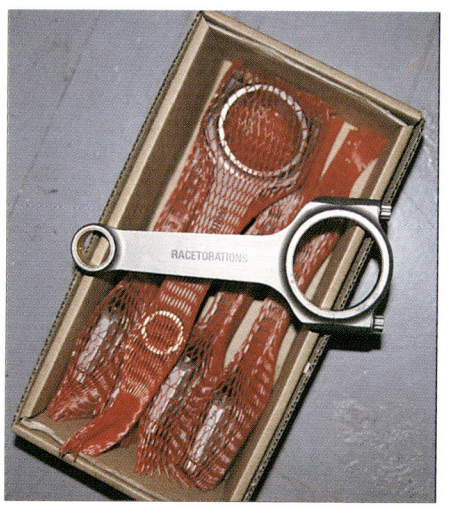

Above & left: Forged pistons, high quality connecting rods and steel cranks are just a few of the engine modifications that need to be carried out by the serious TR6 racer.

This is how the engine and its compartment can look after a car has been through a restorer's hands. You, too, can have an engine like this, but it will cost you lots of money . . .

COLOUR GALLERY

Left: The fuel injection pump, which can be the cause of so much heartache unless it is properly maintained.

COLOUR GALLERY

1969/70 UK sales brochure illustration (captioned "Engineered by Enthusiasts - for Enthusiasts"), shows the lifestyle theme used by Triumph to sell the TR6. The facing page of the brochure shows a young couple arriving at the theatre in 'his' TR6 with the caption "Designed for the man who lives and drives in style."

Designed for the man who lives and drives in style.

New line on power motoring

First thing you'll notice about the new TR6 P.I. is its aggressively simple styling. From the long, low, black grille, flanked by wide-set headlamps, to the dramatically squared off stern, it looks exactly what it is. A powerful, purposeful, no-nonsense, British sports car.

All fussiness has been eliminated. Every line, every curve, every angle earns its keep in terms of better motoring.

That sweeping, aerodynamic bonnet, for instance. It stretches wall to wall and it's hinged at the front, so it won't take off when you're really flying.

All four wings are bolted on. So if you do modify one and don't like the effect, you can go back to our design without having to replace half the body.

Rear lamps, stop lamps, reversing lamps, flashers and reflectors—all these have been integrated into two matching units. Easier to see. Easier to see to.

Everything is practical; even the name badge. You'll never have to scrape dirt and squashed flies from its decorative notches. Because it hasn't any decorative notches.

Equally easy to keep clean are the wheels with their elegant new trim.

O.K., that's the styling picture. Now let's get with the action.

103

COLOUR GALLERY

Petrol injection and the Triumph TR6 P.I.

Petrol injection is a product of international motor racing. It was developed (by Lucas, in this country) to provide Formula One cars with smoother, even more vivid acceleration, with consistent reliability under the most severe driving conditions.

Today, nearly all the top racing cars are fitted with fuel injection. But only a handful of manufacturers offer fuel-injected cars to private motorists.

In Britain, Triumph is the first and only manufacturer to fit petrol injection to a volume production sports car.

How does the system work? In the simplest terms, fuel is pumped from the tank, pressurised and accurately metered. Measured charges are then injected into each port in turn, in the form of a fine spray. They mix with the intake air which is then compressed and ignited in the usual way.

The system is precise, efficient and economical. There is no hit and miss about it; flat spots are eliminated and the engine torque curve is greatly improved.

Teamed with the 2½ litre, six-cylinder TR6 engine, petrol injection gives smoother low-speed motoring, with instant throttle response and searing acceleration, plus cleaner exhaust emission.

The world's top racing drivers rely on fuel injection for extra performance and reliability. Now—as all the best advertisements say—you can, too.

A 150 b.h.p. P.I. engine calls for brakes like these

For real stopping power, the TR6 P.I. has 10¼" discs up front, 9" drum brakes at the rear. Both sets are servo assisted, and will operate independently of each other. Finally, look at that steel girder chassis. It's rigid. Rustproofed. And very, very strong.

Above: Two pages from a 1969/70 UK sales brochure which emphasize the TR6's advanced features.

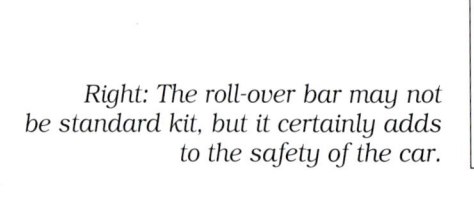

Right: The roll-over bar may not be standard kit, but it certainly adds to the safety of the car.

COLOUR GALLERY

Left: The matt finish to this early car's dashboard is correct, although the steering wheel is wrong.

COLOUR GALLERY

Dramatic front cover of a 1974 UK sales brochure ...

A Triumph you can trust

In the TR6 PI, you're master of a machine that's master of the road.

Put your foot down on the loud pedal and feel the surge – direct petrol injection ensures instant response; move your foot to the stop pedal and the large diameter brakes (discs at the front) are just as obliging. (In the unlikely event of a failure in the hydraulic braking system, the TR's safety-divided brakes ensure that orderly emergency braking may be performed.)

Now, as that leather-covered wheel begins to feel more and more like an old friend, find yourself a corner. Independent suspension, radials, 15" wheels, 5½" J rims and the TR6's wide track and anti-roll bar will all unite to keep you on the curved and narrow.

If you want to let it all hang out on the corners – hard luck, the TR6's roadholding is superb. And that means not only better driving for those with the necessary skill and maturity but also extra safety.

Big, wrap round rearlight clusters, the electrically washed, zone-toughened screen, the absence of reflections (we've even blacked out the arms of the two-speed wipers) – just some small items that make the TR6 PI even more secure. And underneath it all, there's an oh-so-reassuring steel girder chassis.

You can even trust the TR6 PI not to be inconvenient. The simple action wind-and-water-proof hood with its zip-round rear window lets you pick your weather at will. If you choose the hard-top version, that's just as easy to handle.

106

COLOUR GALLERY

... which, inside, still emphasized the exciting lifestyle that went with being a TR6 driver.

COLOUR GALLERY

These pages from the 1975 US sales brochure also have a lifestyle theme, but strongly linked to tradition.

From the land of British Racing Green…

That's where Triumph cars come from! From the land which has produced more world champion cars and drivers in the last twenty years, than any other country. The official international racing color of England is a rich, deep green and so Triumph has introduced to its line of sports cars for 1975, a new finish—British Racing Green. This joins nine other beautiful and bright colors such as Pimento Red below to grace a true and classic sports car like the TR6, a car just as much at home on the race track as on the highway.

108

COLOUR GALLERY

But there is an unusual story about British Racing Green which was born long ago in 1901 when the unlucky number 13 was allotted to English driver Charles Jarrott for the race from Paris to Berlin. In recompense, the French company for which he was driving painted his car green, "a beautiful rich, dark colour," for green was considered a lucky color in France. By the following year Green was accepted as the color for British entries among Blue for France, White for Germany, and Red which at first was America's but soon was awarded to Italy. The American colors became White with blue chassis.

In 1923, the first Triumph car was made and especially in the last 21 years, the era of the TR-series cars, Triumph has come to symbolize "sports car" in America. Of all the Triumphs ever to earn that name, or to wear the hallowed British Racing Green, none does so with more pride or reason than the TR6. TR-type Triumphs have earned their green with class victories and team prizes in such major international events as the Alpine Rally and the 24 Hours of Le Mans.

Today's TR6 bears such hallmarks of its racing heredity as caliper-type front disc brakes (offered first by Triumph), precise-acting rack and pinion steering, a quick-release fuel filler cap, and an overhead-valve twin-carburetor engine.

COLOUR GALLERY

More pages from the 1975 US sales brochure. Here, the would-be TR6 owner's attention is drawn to the car's features. Included is a picture of John McComb's Group 44 car and the brochure's text not only mentions that a TR6 can be used for sports car racing, but that successful competitors might have some of their expenses reimbursed by Triumph!

1. Painted to match the body color, the optional hardtop complements the lines of the TR6 and mates snugly with the roll-up door windows.

2. Long-distance touring in the TR6 is a practical reality thanks to its roomy lockable trunk. The scissors-type jack, tool kit and spare wheel and tire are stowed out of sight beneath the fully carpeted floor panel.

3. Moulded pile carpeting is door-to-door, fitted around the booted shift lever and the console with its controls for the powerful heater-defroster.

4. Bucket seats are deeply pleated in expanded PVC leathercloth, with ventilated seat facings. Both back angle and leg room are adjustable, as is headrest height. Self-locking quick-release catches allow the seat backs to swing forward for access to added storage space behind them.

5. Twin precision-tuned carburetors on a water-heated aluminum intake manifold deliver air and fuel to the straight-six engine of the TR6. Its forged steel crankshaft is carried by four main bearings and fitted with a torsional vibration damper. Valves are overhead, and both the block and head are made of durable chrome-alloy cast iron.

6. Through the padded-rim steering wheel the TR6 driver sees a 7000 rpm tachometer and a matching 5-inch diameter

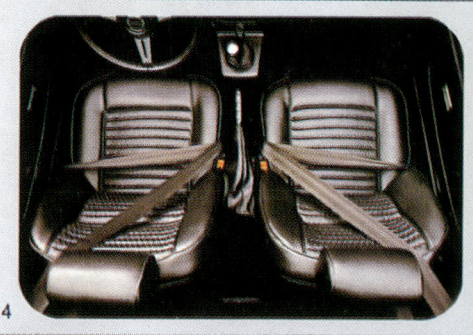

110

COLOUR GALLERY

speedometer with a resettable trip odometer reading to tenths of a mile.

7. Stable, progressive stopping is provided by caliper-type disc brakes on the front wheels. The swept area of the 10.9-inch discs is a generous 233 square inches. A dashboard warning light tells the driver if a failure has occurred in either of the separate front and rear hydraulic brake circuits.

8. TR6—Those initials stand for something. It's an honor to be sixth in the TR series of Triumph sports cars. It stands for 124 miles per hour on the Jabbeke Motorway in Belgium. TR means placing in the top ten at Le Mans, and dominating your class for many years in American road racing.

9. The great tradition of the true convertible is carried on by the TR6 with a rear window that zips down for a flow of fresh air even when the top is up. Transparent plastic quarter windows improve rear vision, and safety is enhanced by a light-reflecting stripe along the edge of the top.

10. Race-prepared TR6's like John McComb's Group 44 car (shown) are formidable competitors in their class in Production Car road racing sanctioned by the Sports Car Club of America. Triumph's Racing Support Program reimburses some of the expenses of successful competitors in this league. With a TR6, suitably modified to meet SCCA regulations, you can enter sports car road racing, one of the most exciting and satisfying new participant sports.

Triumph TR6 Specifications

Engine
In-line 6 cylinder, overhead valves. 4-bearing counterbalanced crankshaft. Exhaust and evaporative emission control. Compression ratio: 7.5 to one. Bore: 2.94 in./74.7 mm. Stroke: 3.74 in./95.0 mm. Displacement: 152 cu. ins./2498 cc. Carburetion: Twin 1.75 in. Stromberg CD2SEV side-draft. Fuel capacity: 11.4 U.S. gallons.

Drive Train
Transmission: manual four-speed with synchromesh on all forward gears. Clutch: 8.5 in. diameter with diaphragm spring, hydraulic operation. Final drive: frame-mounted with hypoid-bevel gears, individual universal-jointed drive shafts to wheels. Overall gear ratios: Reverse 12.47:1, First 11.03:1, Second 7.77:1, Third 5.13:1, Fourth 3.70:1.

Steering
Rack and pinion steering gear. Steering wheel: 14.5 in. dia., three-spoke with padded rim and hub. Turns lock to lock: 3¼. Energy-absorbing steering column.

Suspension
Front: independent, coil springs, anti-roll bar, tubular shock absorbers. Rear: independent, coil springs, piston-type shock absorbers.

Brakes
Dual hydraulic braking systems. Front: 10⅞ in. diameter self-adjusting disc brakes. Rear: 9.0 in. diameter drum brakes.

Road Wheels
Pressed steel, ventilated, 15 x 5.5J rims, fitted with 185SR 15 radial-ply tires.

Dimensions
Wheelbase: 88.0 ins., Front track: 50.3 ins., Rear track: 49.8 ins., Overall length: 162.1 ins., Overall width: 58.0 ins., Overall height: 50.0 ins., Ground clearance: 6.0 ins., Turning circle dia.: 34.0 feet, Basic curb weight: 2422 pounds.

Electrical
Negative-ground 12-volt system. Battery: 57 amp-hr. at 20-hr. rate. Lucas 18ACR 43-amp alternator. Two-speed electric two-blade windshield wipers, self-parking. Twin Lucas windtone horns. Direction indicators, stop and tail lamps, and reversing lamps in rear clusters. Four-way hazard flashers.

Instruments
Speedometer with trip odometer, tachometer, water temperature, battery condition, oil pressure and fuel gauges. Warning lights for high beam, ignition, oil pressure, direction signals, hazard flasher, brake pressure, and seat belts.

Body
Rust-proof steel body on separate steel frame with box-section side members. Bolt-on front and rear fender panels. Forward-hinged hood with interior latch and self-locking support stay. Locking trunk with automatic lid support. Laminated safety glass windshield, winding side windows of toughened safety glass. Folding soft top with fold-down rear window.

Interior
Individual bucket seats trimmed in expanded leathercloth, adjustable back angle and headrest height. Moulded pile carpet with driver heel mat. Three-point inertia reel safety harness. Padded sun visors with passenger-side mirror. Lockable glove compartment with lamp. Padded instrument panel edges; ashtray; recessed door pulls; map pockets; courtesy lights under panel; twin radio speakers on center console.

Color choices
Body colors: Maple, Carmine, Topaz, Pimento, Mimosa, White, French Blue, Delft, British Racing Green, Java. Interior trim colors: Black, Beige, Chestnut and Blue (Topaz, French Blue and Java with Black only).

Options and accessories
Laycock Series J electrically-operated overdrive, operated by a steering column control lever. Gives higher overall gear ratios of 4.09 to one in Third and 2.95 to one in Fourth. Hardtop with fixed rear quarter windows. Door edge guards. AM or AM/FM, or AM/FM MPX radios with 8-track or cassette tape players. Cigarette lighter. Custom-fitted vinyl tonneau cover, chrome or stainless steel luggage rack, ski-carrier adaptors, and luggage protection kits. Lucas driving lamp and/or fog lamp. Rubber floor mats. Walnut gear shift knob. Striping kit in black and silver. Michelin X tires. Special parts and Competition Preparation Manuals for racing available from British Leyland Competition Dept. (Eastern U.S.) 600 Willow Tree Road, Leonia, N.J. 07605, or (Western U.S.) P.O. Box 459, Brisbane, Calif. 94005.

Specifications, colors and prices subject to change without notice.

British Leyland Motors Inc., 600 Willow Tree Road, Leonia, New Jersey 07605.

British Leyland Motors Canada Ltd. 4445 Fairview Street, Burlington, Ont.

COLOUR GALLERY

Above & left: A black wheel centre denotes a CP series car, while satin silver was used for the CR series.

With a lot of hard work and patience, you, too, could have a superb TR6 like Dave Lewis' well-known cup winner.

112

... *Keith Files* ... (Courtesy Richard Dempster)

... *John Whiteley* ... (Courtesy Richard Dempster)

The C & B Championsip Class E cars are a different proposition and bear little relationship to road-going cars. Extensive modifications are allowed to all parts of the car although the original engine cylinder block and head must be used. This is Barry Hodson's beautifully rebuilt aluminium TR6. (Courtesy Richard Dempster)

John Churchill. (Courtesy Richard Dempster)

Joe Henderson. (Courtesy Richard Dempster)

Richard Wright. (Courtesy Richard Dempster)

115

into the red band, the engine's life can be dramatically shortened as a result.

For would-be racers the primary area of attention has to be under the bonnet. Engines can either be rebuilt at home by the knowledgeable mechanic or, alternatively, there are several specialists who know the six cylinder engine inside out. Racetorations, for example, offers a veritable menu ranging from "fast road car" to "full race." At the very least the aim is to give the TR6 the same performance as a modern hot hatch, but it is costly. Tuning an engine properly will not be

Chris May's TR6 takes to the grass at Mallory in an effort to stay ahead during the last round of the Register's '84 Championship.
(Courtesy Fred Scatley)

cheap and for a state of the art, full race specification steel crank engine the outlay will be very substantial. The latter, however, is for the serious racegoer.

20bhp can be gained by fitting a gas-flowed head, a good quality sports exhaust manifold and stainless steel exhaust system and a tune-up on a rolling road. A further 10bhp can be gained by fitting a 357 profile camshaft, stronger valve springs, a sports coil, a modified distributor with the right advance curve and better plugs. The upper limit, though, is still going to be below 250bhp even with an engine stretched to 2.9 litres. For the complete petrol-head while turbocharging is not allowed even in the Modified class, supercharging is.

Beware, though, of fitting a reprofiled cam, follow the advice given in the *TR Driver* and buy from a reputable source as, they say, "there is much trash on the market that is, at best, worse than many a standard cam." The cam used on the 150bhp engine incidentally was numbered 1083 and can be identified by the two rings on its end.

In competition engines standard pistons, even the Powermax AE original, will not last any time, nor will they stand any kind of detonation or mixture problems, high compression or any type of contamination. It is therefore vital to change from cast to forged pistons for serious competition work.

Some of the quicker six cylinder cars still use fuel injection and get round most of the familiar problems by having two metering units, but it is at a cost - typically 3 or 4mpg! A cheaper option is to go for the triple Weber setup.

To keep the car honest in the handling department on the race track the suspension needs to be dramatically stiffened with rock hard springs, all round Spax dampers and composite or very hard rubber bushes. Add to that a set of wider wheels and sensibly

117

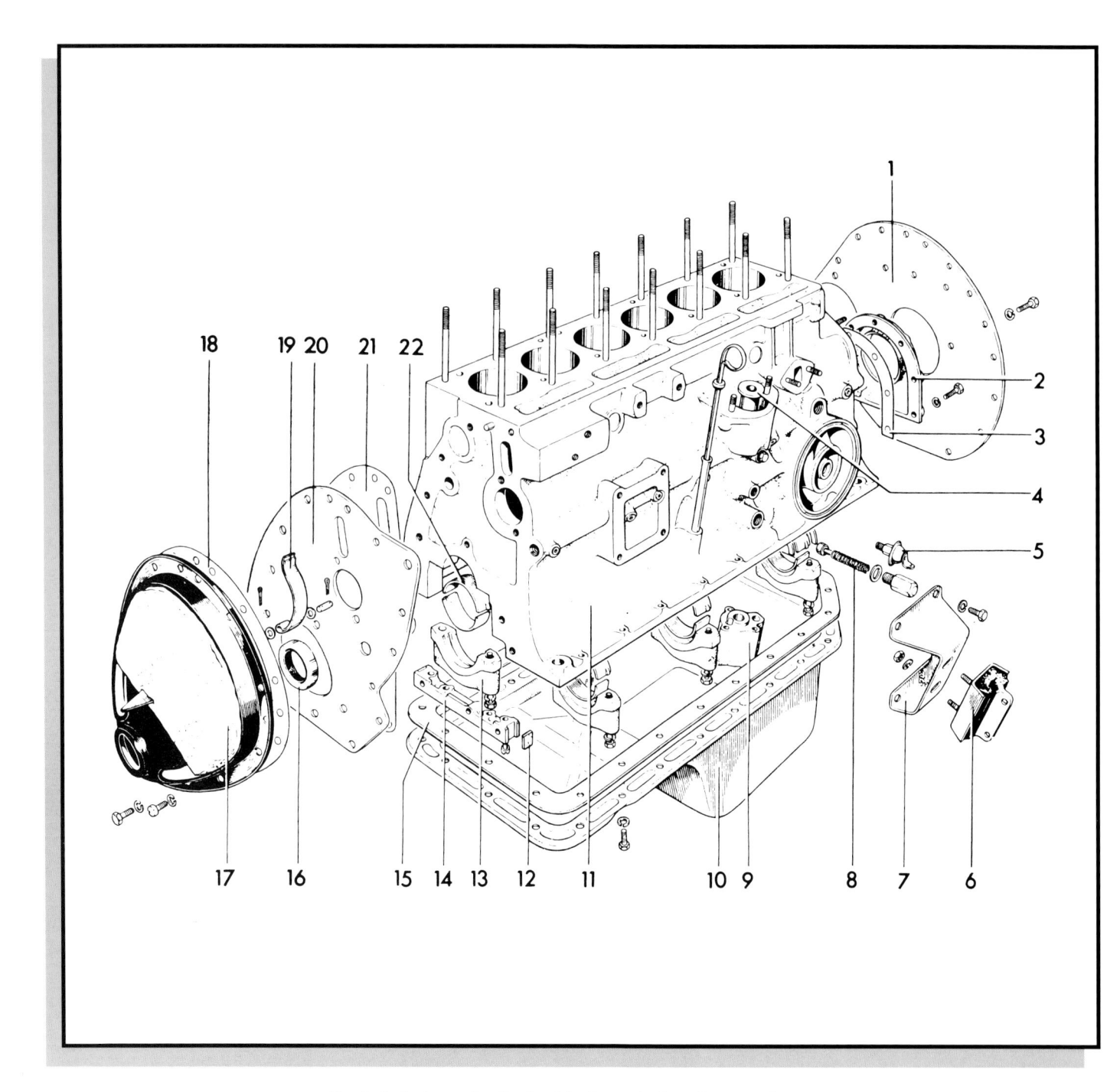

Exploded view of cylinder block, main bearings and sump.

1. Engine backplate.
2. Crankshaft rear oil seal housing.
3. Gasket - crankshaft rear oil seal housing.
4. Bush - oil pump spindle and distributor drive.
5. Oil switch.
6. Engine mounting.
7. Bracket - engine mounting.
8. Relief valve - oil pressure.
9. Body - oil pump.
10. Sump.
11. Cylinder block.
12. Packing - front sealing block.
13. Main bearing cap.
14. Front sealing block.
15. Gasket - sump.
16. Oil seal - timing cover.
17. Timing cover.
18. Gasket - timing cover.
19. Tensioner - timing chain.
20. Engine frontplate.
21. Gasket - engine frontplate.
22. Main bearing shells.

sized modern tyres, such as 185/70s (no bigger than a 195/65), and you'll have a car that is a very effective performer. It also looks better. Some competition TR6s are fitted with rear anti-roll bars but, it should be borne in mind, these are not allowed in the TR Register's Road Sports Championship.

The back axles are relatively problem-free except that it is better to replace the 3.45 ratio with a lower 4.1 as you would otherwise hardly ever get into fourth gear if you assume a 6000rpm limit, which is about 105mph in a TR6 and is realistically about as much as you will see on most circuits. For the roadgoing class, though, the 3.45 ratio must be retained.

A relatively cheap and worthwhile investment is to pick up a spare gearbox from a scrapped Triumph 2000 or 2.5PI. When the time comes it is quite

Above: Ken Lark leads a typically varied field of TRs during the TR Register Championship race at Oulton Park in September 1990.

A TR6 at full pelt as Alan Charlton threads his way through the esses en route to an outright win in the MGCC Thoroughbred Sports Car Championship and Class D honours.

An exploded view of the differential unit.

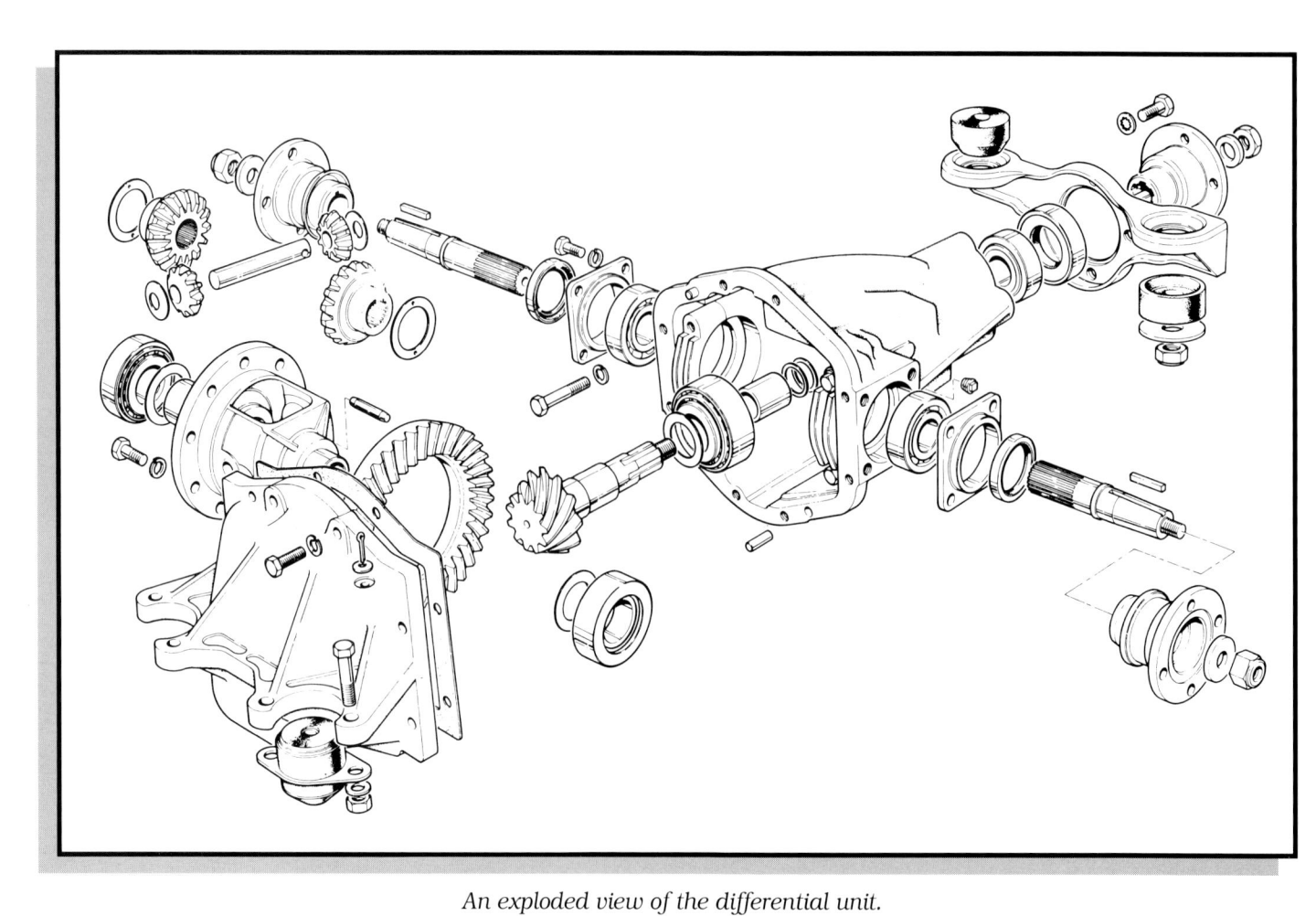

All shapes and sizes in this Championship race as Alan Charlton in his TR6 follows Mike Crosbie's TR4 and Angus McLachlan's TR8.

Rear axle driveshaft and wheel hub carrier.

Below & overleaf: This fully race-prepared TR6 belongs to Steve Clare.

an easy job to install and should take less than a day since it is a straightforward swap. There is no need to touch the internals, although it may be worthwhile strengthening the lay gear and also having a competition-type clutch - which is allowed on even the roadgoing cars - fitted. While some competitors like to have it, overdrive is really an unnecessary luxury.

For competition use, it's a good policy to renew the universal joints in the rear axle and then to keep a very close eye on them. Make sure the hubs and bearings are in good shape too.

When it comes to competition brakes one option is to go for Tarox discs: these have grooves cut into them to reduce fading and, in certain circumstances, enhance braking. The cheaper alternative is ventilated discs which do not cost such an arm and a leg to buy but which are not allowed in any but the Modified class. Beyond this you start talking really big money. Some owners have experimented with unique American made items, but these are really one-offs, while others have opted for either A P Racing's four pot aluminium calipers from saloon racers or 12 inch vented discs with slots. Such braking systems, including the use of carbon-fibre pads, utterly transform the car's braking characteristics but are only to be found on the very serious competition car.

At the rear, one option is to go for Alfin-type drums which featured lateral rather than radial fins. The trouble is that these items have long been out of production (although it is possible to find replicas) and they are not particularly attractive. It is not permissible to fit discs on the rear axle, even on cars running in the Modified class.

Finding the right competition brake shoe is also proving to be difficult. Originally VG95 used to be the benchmark but is now extremely difficult to find with the result that British specialists like Racetorations are looking to import special material from the United States.

Naturally a race-bred brake fluid will be required and Castrol Racing Fluid is the most widely used. Its high boiling point leads to less brake-fade. The use of normal fluid will quickly result in the brakes becoming nonexistent, usually when you most need them.

Fuel tanks are a problem with the

TR6s can provide sprinting and hillclimbing fun, too. Here's Graham Cooper on the startline of the Rumster Hillclimb in Scotland ...

... and the same car making smoke at Arran Wye in 1985.

A line-up of TR6s which, although race-prepared, are still road legal.

Some intrepid owners are even prepared to go drag racing. This TR6 is pictured at Santa Pod.

later TR6s in that the baffling for the injection cars and the CAV-type filter bowl often cause an inexplicable fuel cut-out on certain corners and it is very difficult to fix. It may only be momentarily that the engine dies and then coughs, splutters and hiccups before picking up again when in a straight line, but it is most frustrating when having a close dice with another car. One answer is not to run the car with the fuel tank less than half full although, of course, it is at the expense of weight. An aluminium petrol tank with FIA-approved foam should be fitted for the serious racer and the fuel lines re-routed away from the exhaust pipe.

In the furtherance of weight reduction you may want to replace the original steel exterior panels with lighter glassfibre or alloy panels and remove the bumpers and overriders. The removal of interior panels, though, is prohibited in every class.

As can be seen, just getting your competition driving licence and registering for a championship is but the tip of what is usually an expensive iceberg. However, sprints, hillclimbs, racing and rallying provide a great deal of entertainment and fun for very many people and, if you are going to do it, there are few cars that can offer as much fun as a well sorted TR6.

VII
CONCLUSIONS OF THE FOURTH ESTATE

What they said

"Indomitable in defeat; indifferent in victory - it has traditionally taken a crisis to bring out the best in the British," stated the American magazine *Car and Driver* on driving the TR6 for the first time as reported in the February 1969 issue. It was a piece which extolled the virtues of the car while slyly poking fun at the British for their celebration of major defeats. "The Englishman celebrates The Crimea and the Relief of Mafeking in his gentleman's club, and toasts the anniversary of Dunkirk. Defeats all. But undiminished in their glory.

"It is little wonder then, that the British have warmed to their discomfort cars; have seen sales dip in the US; have built even *more* discomfort cars and have seen those sales slip even further. It is all part of the morality play, of a piece with the mannerly sadism of the British public school with its dank halls and medieval treatment of the child that he might suffer inestimable discomfort only to be able to gauge opulence better when he attains his majority.

"How, one wonders, is the Englishman ever going to cope with the TR6? Hopefully in the same way as his ancestor survived Trafalgar, the War of 1812, and how he, himself, was able to dip deep into his reserve of emotional strength and with grit and determination live through the awful moments of victory at the end of World War II.

"Crisis is upon him again. The terrible truth will dawn soon enough; and when it does we will see if the Englishman is up to it. The TR6, we are moved to report (only grateful that we can report it from the safety of these shores), is an excellent automobile. It is bluff and straightforward - as its precedents have been - but it is no longer Colonel Blimp. Subtlety has crept into British Eden, and the protectorate is the better for it. Still bereft of the fuel injection which made its British counterpart, the TR5, an energetic car beyond the dreams of US Triumph owners, the new car is nonetheless the fastest, most comfortable, best-mannered Triumph ever to offer enchantment to the American buyer."

This was the kind of review about which PR departments dream, especially as it was in the all-important American market, but *Car and Driver* was not the only magazine impressed with the car.

"It's the kind of car for which a young man could give his eye-teeth," said the July 1969 edition of *Popular Imported Cars*. "Like a beautiful woman, the TR6 is the sort of creature you like to be close to and to be seen with. Certainly it's sexy - there's no denying it, and what's more it's accented with a very British flair that makes it all the more interesting. The appearance, though updated slightly this year, nevertheless is steeped in an old tradition of English road machines, but still with a penchant for fun loving and carelessness that's as exciting as Fanny Hill."

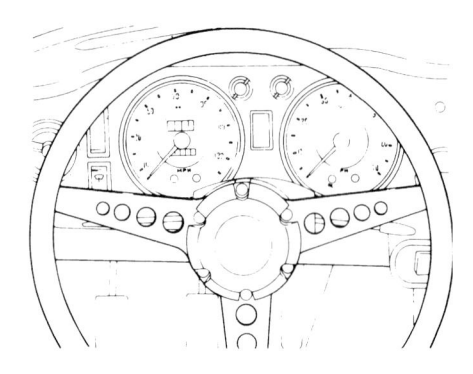

In comparison to such glowing words, those of *Road & Track* seemed tame. "Triumph surprised us with the TR6," reported the February 1969 issue of the magazine. "We've been hoping for an all-new sports car from them for some time, but what they've done is update the old one again. This time there's new sheet metal, the car having received a 6-cyl engine earlier to become the TR5 (home market) or TR250 (US)."

"The TR series has gradually progressed to the point where the healthy straight six engine, well mannered four-speed transmission, fierce braking system and well thought out package render it a best buy for the dollar, particularly for that type of enthusiast driver who feels that he does not have a sports car unless he enjoys lots of wind in his face," reported the February 1969 issue of *Road Test*. "The TR6 looks like an honest two-seater, suitable for touring and ready for serious competition at an instant's notice. And that's what it is. Considerable effort has been expended upon interior finishings, resulting in a comfortable and attractive environment. Yet," the report continues, "the TR6 can be counted upon to be one of the strongest competitors in the viciously competitive SCCA 'C' production class when the first green flag falls in '69."

The British press was a little more sanguine in its appraisal of the new model and spent more time devoting itself to the difference between the TR5 and the TR6. "From all angles the TR6 looks quite different from the TR5," stated *Motor* in the January 18 1969 issue while *Autocar* in the January 16 1969 issue pointed out that "the TR4/5 body shape is surprisingly old" and that "the introduction of the six-cylinder engine has rendered the prominent power bulge unnecessary and cleared the way for a major facelift."

When it came to the first comprehensive road tests, though, the adjectives were far more flowing. In its road test of April 17 1969 *Autocar*'s opening paragraph waxed lyrical about the merits of the car, although it saw it in a different light to *Car and Driver*.

"Even if the Austin-Healey 3000 had not been dropped, the TR6 would have taken over as the he-man's sports car in its own right. It is very much a masculine machine, calling for beefy muscles, bold decisions and even ruthlessness on occasions. It could be dubbed the last of the *real* sports cars, because it displays many qualities so beloved in vintage times. In spite of all this (although many would say because), it is a tremendously exhilarating car to drive."

The *Motor* was a little more down to earth in its opening remarks, as published in the June 7 1969 issue. "While some other mass production sports cars become gradually tamer and outperformed and outhandled by an ever faster rash of sporting saloons, the Triumph TR has stood apart from the common herd. In its latest form the TR6 represents what is probably the best value for money in open top terms. Its predecessor, the TR5, set the pace with the stretched Triumph six-cylinder unit mated to Lucas fuel injection which gave a combination of real punch and mechanical refinement and a specification that could only be matched by more expensive machinery. The 6 is more than just a face-lifted 5; the standard TR5 chassis, its inner structure and the doors are retained but new outer panels styled by Karmann-Ghia provide a very real transformation which is more than just skin deep. A slightly bigger boot is possible with the squared-off tail and the seats have been re-shaped but there is no more room behind them for the occasional short term 'collapsible' adult. For two, though, the TR6 is a comfortable well-appointed car to ride in."

In the US, the July 1969 issue of *Popular Imported Cars* agreed with the latter. "The seats are wonderful and a vast improvement over the flat 'chairs' in the TR4. We particularly like the solution to the head restraint problem. The restraint is an extension of the seatback, but is hinged and can be folded forward when the tonneau cover is in place. The seats are ventilated and support the body from the lower thigh all the way to the back of the head. This kind of comfort goes a long way toward reducing driver fatigue."

Road Test magazine agreed about the seats, as reported in its January 1970 issue: "The seats are extremely comfortable buckets; once you're belted in, you *know* you're not going to bounce around no matter what happens. The seats slide forward and back on surprisingly long tracks. Our six-footers were able to get the seat so far back that they could just barely get the clutch all the way to the floor with the tip of the shoe. The majority of the spacing is due to the firewall being well forward of the dash. Even with the seat well back, it isn't possible to do real, honest-to-goodness Italian-style arms-out driving.

"The hydraulic clutch on the TR6 is pretty fierce," the report continued, "and takes a day or so to get used to. It is difficult to actually stall the rugged engine, but you'll get some jerky starts and gear changes until you establish the clutch and throttle synchronization firmly in your reflex patterns. The four-speed, all-synchro transmission is smooth, but takes a very firm hand for neat shifting. Triumph has never been known for the light knife-through-butter shifting of the MGs or Porsches."

Motor agreed. In its June 7 1969 report it said: "The gear change on this car was notchy and obstructive, particularly into first and second when the oil was cold; several attempts were sometimes needed to engage first at rest. With firm deliberate movements, though, changes could be made quite smoothly, especially as the throttle movement seemed less floppy than that on other Triumphs. The clutch gripped smoothly and well but was very heavy to push, 52lb being quite demanding in traffic."

Ray Hutton, the respected motoring journalist, liked the overdrive, though, and commented in the November 1969 issue of *Motor Racing and Sportscar* that: "The optional overdrive which operates on top, third and second gears has long been one of the most likeable features of the TR range. Engaged by a steering column stalk, the selection of seven ratios means that there is always one that is exactly right for the conditions. In practice, stop-start traffic encourages use of 2nd and 2nd overdrive, fast winding roads are just right for third and its higher ratio and of course overdrive top gives relaxed cruising on motorways; 100mph represents only 3860rpm. The gearchange itself is quite heavy, notchy and positive, if not of the quickest; a few years ago it might have been excellent, but recent Ford products have set the standards by which these things must be judged. Some of that man-sized energy is needed for clutch though, which is nonetheless smooth in operation."

The February 1970 issue of the Australian magazine *Wheels* also commented on the clutch operation. "The he-man masculinity can be carried too far and Triumph has gone overboard with the clutch, gearchange operation. Inching forward in traffic would soon give you the quadriceps of a front row forward. Now heavy or competition clutches are not to be maligned if they do the job and mostly that means giving progressive and positive control. But the TR6's feels too taut and unrelenting. Smooth changes without any transmission train snatch require a lot of concentration and the snatch that does occur is in no way blameable on the sweet engine. The shift likes to be pulled through sharply and needs a semi-race technique of using a full power take-up after changing to smooth the change. But even if the shift is stiff, notchy and hard to use, the ratios are well spaced and filled by the overdrive for those not satisfied."

The December 1969 issue of *Australian Motor Manual* found the car wanting. "Performancewise, it's a disappointment to those who have experienced the sweet power of the now-departed TR5... Whereas the TR5's performance was shattering by any standards," it continues, "the heavier TR6 only just keeps pace with the current crop of V8s and is actually slower in acceleration than the 2.5PI sedan."

This was not a view shared by Ray Hutton. "Performance has gone well beyond the Healey," he commented in the *Motor Racing and Sportscar* article, "making the TR6 one of the most rapid cars in both the 2.5 litre capacity class and in its price category.... Furthermore the fuel injection engine has a good deal of punch throughout its rev range and excellent throttle response, accompanied by a most pleasing bark from its twin exhaust pipes. Unlike some fuel injection installations we have tried, starting from cold doesn't present any problems; there is a sort of choke or enrichening device which needs to be pushed home almost immediately the engine has fired. When warm the tickover runs at a slightly lumpy 700-800rpm."

The bark of the exhausts was also picked up by *Road Test* magazine in its January 1970 report. "Triumph has avoided one current trend in sports cars that has annoyed many old-line *aficionados*: quiet exhaust pipes. In the concept of the true sports car, a machine that revels in being mechanically superb, and which uses its horsepower in the most efficient ways possible, the sound of that power being used is extremely important. There is nothing duller than driving a sports car that purrs softly. That's not playing the game, and it is indeed a game. The

TR6 has two giant pipes jutting to the rear, and they blat out a wonderful sound of high-revving power. At stop lights you find yourself blipping the throttle, not to challenge other drivers to a drag race (where you'd lose, likely as not) but just for the sweet sounds. With the TR6's all-synchro box, there is really no reason for double-clutching for down shifts, but it sounds so great that you find yourself doing so even when it really isn't necessary to drop a gear."

Conversely the February 1972 report on the TR6 in *Hot Car* magazine found it to be very quiet. "The TR6 is one of the very few soft top sports cars around that allows you to listen to the radio at 100mph."

What the magazine did not like, however, was the heating and demisting. "Despite the presence of swivelling vents at the ends of the facia," it said, "and a two-speed blower the system proved to be quite useless. Heat output was minimal and the demister didn't. We haven't heard any similar complaints from drivers of other Sixes," it conceded, "so assume it was a fault particular to this test car."

"What the TR6 really needs," suggested *Cars and Car Conversions* of March 1971, "is a decent navigator's light, or a number plate light fixed to the dashboard like the MGB," while the *Australian Motor Manual* stated that "Heater controls on the TR6 are less easy to use than they should - and could - be." Its compatriot publication *Sports Car World* took things a stage further by complaining about scuttle shake in its May 1971 report and disliked the position of the fuel filler cap. "At the risk of being petty," it said, "we would suggest that perhaps putting the fuel filler cap in the middle of the front of the rear deck was probably not a good idea - every second service station driveway attendant manages to slop petrol all over the rear deck trying to fuel the car!"

At least, though, they liked the hood. "The hood is truly a thing of beauty - one of the best sports car hoods in a long while. Apart from the easy erection and folding down, it exhibits no flapping at any speed, and does nothing to detract from the lines of the car. It is beautifully watertight - the only water that defeated it was the high-pressure jets in the automatic car wash, and they're hardly normal!"

When it came to handling, most of the reports were kind but pointed out that it had its foibles. "The ride is pleasant," reported *Road Test* magazine on its introduction to the car in February 1969, "although the TR6 won't let the driver remain unaware of the road surface on bumpy cobblestone byways. Cornering with the fully independent suspension is of the order expected of cars which command twice the price," the magazine enthused.

"The addition of a front anti-roll bar . . . combined with wheels that are an inch wider," reported the February 1969 issue of *Road & Track*, "and the optional Michelin X tires (as on our test car) gives high speed cornering stability and bite that is new to the big TR. From about 45mph up the cornering response is quite neutral, and lifting the throttle foot in a hard turn brings the tail out gently. When the going gets rough, the TR's independent rear suspension - which was cobbled into a car designed for a live axle - is less happy than most systems. The frame rails actually run *underneath* its axles, severely limiting suspension travel in the rebound direction. The result is a strange combination of softness in the bounce (up) direction and super-control on the rebound - as if a big strap were keeping you from leaving the ground - the point being to get a decent ride and avoid contact between the axles and those rails underneath them. Under conditions that don't use up the rebound travel, the normal advantages of irs [independent rear suspension] - namely the ability to corner on bumpy surfaces without losing adhesion - do apply to the TR6."

Despite the extra power of the injection cars, *Motor* magazine had a similar view: "The handling, too, has been improved a little and it feels as though the present body imparts a little more stiffness to the separate chassis than previously. A stiffer front anti-roll bar and rims an inch wider than before at 5.5J combat the power-off-tuck-in of the TR5 which required rather quick correction. It works; the car handles well with high cornering powers on wet, dry and bumpy surfaces. In fact the TR6 has a nice blend of old he-man feel and up-to-date behaviour."

Ray Hutton concurred in his report for the November 1969 issue of *Motor Racing and Sportscar*. "In the roadholding department things have improved drastically since the cart-sprung days. Weight transfer provides some dramatic tail-down attitudes on acceleration and, under some circumstances, during hard cornering but the relatively unsophisticated rear end does a good job in keeping the rear wheels in adhesion. With its chunky Michelin XAS radials it is difficult to induce wheelspin from take-off and the car understeers pretty well all through the range. A tail-out attitude in the dry is almost impossible and even in the wet, when the throttle needs to be treated with a little more care, the rear end holds its line very well. The ride is firm, but acceptable, with undulating roads showing up effective damping. Body roll is negligible. On bad surfaces like a rough pave there is quite a lot of moaning and groaning from the steering, suspension and chassis but the car remains directionally stable. The steering itself is good, if a little low-geared, but gives a good lock for a car of this type."

The American magazine *Sports Car World*, however, took a different view. "Easily the worst handling sports or performance car we have ever driven," it said in its January 1973 report when comparing it with a Datsun 240Z. "The car bump steers nastily, with the front skipping well and truly off line in any corner with a trace of irregularity. It is also a dogged understeerer, with blanc-mange response to throttle control so that trying to counteract the understeer coming into the bend is usually a battle of Napoleonic magnitude.

"If you decide not to worry about getting rid of it and go into the bend in understeer - or just come in too damned fast anyway - the front wheels let go entirely and you're in a full front-end slide. Only in the wet have I ever had this happen in any other car.

"In certain bends, particularly long, fast, slightly downhill curves, backing off the throttle suddenly produces very drastic results - the tail whips out into oversteer, and you'll need to be quick to catch it. This can be anticipated and used to advantage though. But I can't see that you'd ever learn to live with the bump steer or understeer slides - you'd just have to give up any pretensions of having a sporty car in the bends."

So in the final analysis how did the TR6 fare against the 240Z? "Really, the TR6 is just a poor tired old thing with a ruggedly handsome body and a beautiful engine. With time and trouble and Koni shockers in the front you might be able to sort out the handling to at least make it reasonable. But what can you do about scuttle shake that's so bad I realised I didn't know what the word meant until I drove a TR?

"The Z is basically an infinitely better motor car, although it has its problems with that poorly-developed front end, tasteless plasticky trim and a noisy rear suspension that's harder than it should be."

Nil points for the Triumph as far as this reviewer was concerned. The British magazine *Custom Car* compared the TR6 to a 3-litre Ford Capri (a V6-engined car) in its May 1972 issue, the reviewer obviously having his heart in the right place commenting on the TR6 that he "could go zooming around in summer and impress all the chicks," while a colleague in the same review commented that while he preferred the Ford it was "reluctantly because that TR engine is really fabulous and deserves a better vehicle." He then added, somewhat prophetically: "Leyland must do something radical soon for a replacement if they are ever to stay in America. Despite the success of the Super Coupé thing, I do feel that sports cars have a future in Britain but they must lead in design and performance."

What Car? carried out a group car test which pitted the TR6 against the MGB, Caterham Seven, Jensen-Healey and Morgan Plus 8 in April 1974 and in its typically thorough way examined each model in minute detail. Its conclusion, though, was more woolly than normal.

"The Morgan and Lotus (Caterham) are tremendous fun in the right circumstances. On smooth roads in dry conditions they are really thrilling to drive fast but they lose most of their appeal on the open road at a steady 50mph, for they offer few creature comforts. Further, you will have to wait at least two years for a Morgan.

"The Morgan has a bone-shaking ride, incredibly heavy steering, cramped accommodation and make-shift weather protection. The shattering performance tends to make up for this in some respect but the occupants tend to arrive at the end of a journey feeling completely worn out. The Lotus is far more civilised but it too leaps from bump to bump, rattles and bangs and gives the occupants a hard time.

"The MGB, TR6 and Jensen-Healey

cannot hope to match the performance of the Lotus and Morgan but they offer the sort of equipment, accommodation and standard of trim that most people will need if they are to live with the car every day. The TR6 is beginning to feel its age, for the chassis is too flexible, the ride hard, the steering heavy and accommodation more cramped than on the other two. The persistent stories of unreliability in the fuel injection system cannot be ignored either."

In the end the What *Car?* team opts for the MGB on account of it being £600 less than the Jensen and nearly £300 less than the Triumph.

What they say now

TR6s are now a staple diet of all the classic car magazines. It took a while for the model to be accepted as such, but TR6s are now a part of the fold. It is not difficult to find advice, technical tips, routine maintenance and specialist services and so while the TR6 has become older it has become easier to look after. Matt White in the Winter 1993 issue of *British Cars* magazine managed to convey the right kind of flavour of what the model means to today's journalists in his article entitled "Last of the Truly Great Sportscars" which is here reprinted in full.

"Triumph Roadster. The abbreviation TR has been applied to the company's' sportscars since the TR1 prototype spawned the hugely successful TR2. The TR range of sportscars were designed from the outset with the magical figure of 100mph in mind: 100mph and availability at a reasonable cost. The TR2 was, after all, on sale for around £900 in 1953.

"The TR2's 4-cylinder, wet liner 1991cc engine produced 90bhp at 4800rpm. Road testers' reports at the time quoted between 103 and 105mph. Testers were ecstatic about such performance being 'within the reach of the man of moderate means. . . . '"

"So, having set the precedent of speed, Triumph continued with it up to the last true TR - the 6. The striking and perhaps rather gaunt front of the TR6 has always been noticeable. The design was honed to become less of the bone shaker and more of the refined, smooth sports car expected by the motorist of the late Sixties.

"The TR6 closed the doors on a sporting car tradition that we in Britain did rather well. They were fairly basic drivers' cars that, in a taut package, delivered power and speed, unrivalled open air touring and the look of a purposeful sports machine. Sport it certainly was. People didn't buy the TR6 just to get from A to B. They wanted to have fun getting there.

"When I passed my driving test, aged seventeen, and was given the road to terrorise, there was one car I really, really wanted - the new Triumph TR6. I would even put up with that awful plum paintwork, (it's called Damson I am told) just so long as I could slide behind that nifty three-spoke steering wheel, start that magnificent sounding 6-cylinder engine and screech away, the requisite flared trousered blonde by my side.

"In reality, the first car I ever owned was a 1958 Morris Minor. I say owned, but in fact it was only mine until a deep, cunningly disguised ditch, on a sharp bend just outside Epping, claimed it, one dark night, five days later. At least I am still here to be able to say I learnt my lessons early. And it could have been worse - it could have been a brand new, plum coloured TR6.

"The trouble was, I kept seeing them everywhere. In addition, when they were parked, you could have a good look at all the controls and twiddly bits, there being no roof to interrupt the view. The 'Injection' badge at the back increased the mystique, as did the discovery that it had 'Overdrive', whatever that was.

"Even though my youthful yearnings were never fulfilled, I have always maintained a soft spot for the TR6. The TR5 or 4 are perhaps more 'classic' in appearance but the TR6 was a new car when I was growing up, and as such was the one I noticed.

"To learn more about the TR6, I spoke to Derek Pollock, Secretary of North London's Club Triumph and editor of *Club Torque*, their club magazine.

"In the mid-Sixties, Triumph, realising firstly that there was still a considerable market for traditional sports cars in America, and secondly that that market near enough demanded a new shape of car every year or so, were in the unenviable position of having to produce a new model cheaply, based on the TR5 framework as much as possible.

"Giovanni Michelotti - the designer of the TR4 to 5 models - was fully employed on other British Leyland projects at the time and the brief went to the firm of Wilhelm Karmann GmbH, who had recently expanded and were looking for new projects. Michelotti was also only a design house and Triumph needed a company able to make the body tooling as well. The clincher as far as Karmann were concerned, was that they could do all this themselves. In effect, this most British of sportscars was the work of a German company developing the original Italian styling to suit American tastes. But no camel ever looked like this.

"Working to a tight schedule and even tighter budget, Karmann succeeded in producing the handsome and modern TR6 design, cleverly maintaining the TR5 base unit of floor, scuttle, screen and doors and inner panels but making new wings, bonnet and bootlid and new front and rear panels. It was ready to start production in late 1968 after only a fourteen month development time, a time which included the necessity of producing two sets of drawings for everything as the Germans worked in metric and the British in imperial measurements in those pre-computer days!

"Cars for the USA had twin Stromberg carburettors fitted to satisfy the stringent Federal anti-smog regulations, and these gave 126bhp, but cars in Britain were fitted with Lucas fuel injection, which boosted this figure to 142bhp. The TR6 engine, a 2498cc overhead cam 6-cylinder unit as fitted to the TR5, was, with the aid of fuel injection, able to return a top speed of 120mph. The four-speed, all synchromesh gearbox could be fitted with Laycock de Normanville overdrive as an option which acted on second, third and fourth gears and later just third and fourth. Effectively a six or seven gear transmission, this gave the TR6 enormous flexibility and long-legged cruising ability.

"The neat dashboard of wood veneer displayed all the car's functions and a minimum of switchgear made the interior simple but well laid out. The high-back bucket seats, which were newly introduced on the TR6 to comply with Federal safety requirements, were PVC trimmed with excellent restraint for sideways movement. The stow-away hood was simple to operate and well made.

"At the design stage the rear was the result of much thought by Karmann. Mirroring the flat surface of the bonnet, the boot was also given a flat surface and then squared off at the end with what came to be known as a Kamm-type tail after the German engineer who developed this aerodynamic device. It would go on to become a trademark copied by several other manufacturers. The magnetic filler cap remained in the centre of the deck to allow for filling from either side of the car while wraparound lamp assemblies enhanced the car's aggressive look.

"The end result was a decent sized boot, fully carpeted for the first time, which was increased in size to 6.1 cubic feet, but in opening from the top it presented a high lip for cases to be hauled over. The spare wheel was located in a well underneath the floor and also secreted in the boot was the pumpgear for the injection unit.

"Rostyle wheel trims were initially introduced onto the car but they were really quite unsuited and were dropped early in the model's life. They were replaced by good looking pressed steel wheels with a matt black plastic centre with the TR6 motif, although wire wheels with a hexagonal centre nut could always be specified as an option.

"Tyres were 165HR-15 radials, and with independent coil springs all round, give the car good adhesion but with some understeer which the road testers of the time commented on. In fact great effort went into improving the TR's road manners. An anti-roll bar, 0.625-inch thick, was fitted at the front and one inch wider wheels increased the overall track by 1 inch."

APPENDIX I

SPECIALISTS & CLUBS

SPECIALISTS

Belgium
Belgian British Car,
15 Grand'route Bte 2,
1435 Corbais (Mont St. Guibert).
Tel: (10) 658076
Fax: (10) 659297

France
Bastuck & Co France,
18A Chemin des Dames,
57500 Saint-Avold.
Tel: 87929444
Fax: 87929445

Betaset,
25 rue F. Brean,
78790 Septeuil.
Tel: (1) 30938502
Fax: (1) 30934077

Spitsfit,
62 rue magenta,
69100 Villeurbanne.
Tel: 78858711
Fax: 78846740

UK
Bank Top Garage,
Stepney Bank,
Newcastle-Upon-Tyne,
Tyne & Wear NE26 1AL.
Tel: 0191 2610979
Specialists in classic car restoration from running repairs to major rebuilds. Also recovery and storage service.

Beech Hill Garage,
Beech Hill,
Reading,
Berks RG7 2AU.
Tel: 01734 884774
Fax: 01734 884864
TR spares, servicing and MOT work.

British Motor Industry Heritage Trust Ltd.,
Heritage Motor Centre,
Banbury Road,
Gaydon,
Warwickshire CV35 0BJ.
Tel: 01926 641188
Fax: 01926 641555
Manufacturer and supplier of genuine parts made from original tooling, including bodyshells for TR6.

Broadfield Classics,
Unit 3,
Broadfield Farm,
Great Somerford,
Nr. Chippenham,
Wiltshire SN15 5EL.
Tel: 01249 720070
Fax: 01249 892008
Triumph restorers.

Central Triumph,
96-102 Occupation Lane,
Woodville,
Swadlicote,
Derbyshire DE11 8EX.
Tel: 01283 551618

Chestnut Classics,
Old Station Yard,
Barnack,
Stamford,
Lincs PE9 3DW.
Tel: 01780 740303
Fax: 01780 740945

Classic Triumph Spares,
Timbertop Farm,
Maidstone Road,
Sidcup,
Kent DA14 5AR.

Cox & Buckles Spares,
991 Wolverhampton Road,
Oldbury,
West Midlands B69 4RJ.

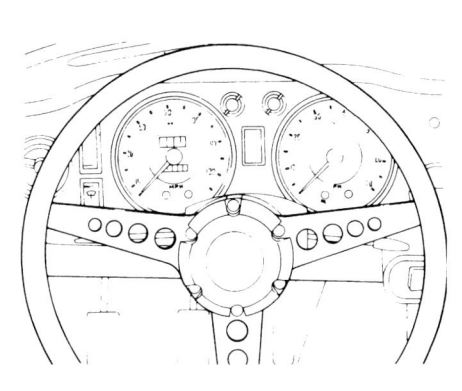

Tel: 0121 544 5555
Fax: 0121 544 4340
British Motor Heritage approved distributor of quality parts for all Triumph TR models.

Cox & Buckles Spares,
22-28 Manor Road,
Richmond,
Surrey TW9 1YB.
Tel: 0181 948 6666
Fax: 0181 940 9268
British Motor Heritage approved distributor of quality parts for all Triumph TR models.

Cox & Perry
Frettenham Road,
Horstead,
Coltishall,
Norwich,
Norfolk NR13 6RS.
Tel: 01603 737195
Specialist in classic car restoration from running repairs to total rebuilds.

TD Fitchett,
Fitchett (Redland Industrial Estate),
Station Hill,
Oakengates,
Telford,
Shropshire TF2 9AA.
Parts stocked for all Triumph models and re-manufacturer of parts from original factory tooling.

Moss Europe Ltd.,
Victoria Villas,
Richmond,
Surrey TW9 2JX.
Tel: 0181 948 8888
Fax: 0181 940 0484

Moss Europe Ltd.,
15 Allington Way,
Yarm Road Industrial Estate,
Darlington,
Co. Durham DL1 4QB.
Tel: 01325 281343
Fax: 01325 485563

Northern TR Centre,
Sedgefield Industrial Estate,
Sedgeland,
Cleveland TS21 3EE.
Tel: 01740 621447
Fax: 01740 622873
Specialist in all aspects of Triumph sports cars. Parts available either new or secondhand. Complete restorations.

Quiller Triumph,
Units 12-13,
Wrights Yard,

Canton Road,
Bromley,
Kent BR1 2SN.
Tel: 0181 464 1386
Triumph-only specialist from full servicing to repairs and modifications.

Racetorations,
Sandars Road,
Gainsborough,
Lincolnshire DN21 1RZ
Tel: 01427 616565
Restoration and mechanical rebuilding of TR2-6s plus full range of spares.

Revington TR, (aka TR Spares SW)
Home Farm,
Middlezoy,
Somerset TA7 0PD.
Tel: 01823 698437
Fax: 01823 698109

Rimmer Bros.,
Triumph House,
Sleaford Road,
Bracebridge Heath,
Lincoln LN4 2NA.
Tel: 01522 568000
Fax: 01522 567000

Six Spares,
Rear of 140c Heath Road,
Twickenham,
Middx. TW1 4BN.
Tel: 0181 892 1041
Fax: 0181 891 5567
Range of spares for all Triumph models.

Southern Triumph Spares,
11A Stamford Road,
Southborne,
Bournemouth,
Dorset BH6 5DP.
Tel: 01202 423687
Fax: 01202 427008
A small restoration company. Many secondhand parts and most new service items.

STR Engineering and Preparation,
1 Beverley Avenue,
West Mersea,
Essex CO5 8EU.
Tel & fax: 01206 386001

T&M Classics,
Waterlands Farm,
Chinnor Road,
Thame,
Oxon OX9 3RE.
Tel: 01844 261712

TR Bitz,
Lyncastle Way,
Barley Castle Trading Estate,
Appleton,
Warrington,
Cheshire WA4 4ST.
Tel: 01925 861861
Fax: 01925 860816
Triumph TR and spares for sale.

TR Enterprises,
Dale Lane,
Blidworth,
Notts NG21 0SA.
Tel: 01623 793807
Fax: 01623 799043
All aspects of servicing, repairs and restoration undertaken.

TR GB.
Unit 1,
Sycamore Farm Industrial Estate,
Long Drove,
Somersham,
Huntingdon,
Cambs PE17 3HW.
Tel: 01487 842168
Fax: 01487 740274
TR specialist. Full range of new and secondhand spares.

TR Shop Limited,
16 Chiswick High Road,
London W14 1TH.
Tel: 0181 995 6621
Fax: 0181 742 1284
TR parts supplier.

TR Workshop Ltd.,
The Steadings,
Tetbury Road,
Cirencester,
Glos GL67 6PX.
Tel: 01285 659900
Fax: 01285 659900
TR specialist. Workshop and full range of spares.

Triumph Care,
Crown Works,
1 Church Road,
Norbiton,
Kingston-upon-Thames,
Surrey KT1 3DB.
Tel: 0181 549 9305
Fax: 0181 541 0403
Car sales, rustproofing, servicing and MOT, welding and repairs. New and secondhand spares.

Triumph Restorations,
Swansea.

Tel: 01792 580564
Restoration and servicing for Triumphs.

Triumph Tune,
22-28 Manor Road,
Richmond,
Surrey TW9 1YB.
Tel: 0181 948 6668
Fax: 0181 940 9268
Tuning and performance parts including tuning components and suspension kits.

USA
BritFab,
PO Box 8315,
Greensboro,
NC 27419.

British Parts Northwest,
4105 SE. Lafayette Hwy.,
Dayton,
OR 97114.
Tel: 503 864 2001
Fax: 503 864 2081

Moss Motors Ltd.,
7200 Hollister Ave.,
PO Box 847,
Goleta,
California 93116.
Tel: 805 968 1040
Fax: 805 968 6910

Special Interest Car Parts,
1340 Hartford Avenue,
Johnston,
Rhode Island 02919.
Tel: 401 831 8850

CLUBS
Australia
TR Register Australia Inc.,
International Liaison: Bob Slender,
125 Eaton Road,
West Pennant Hills,
NSW 2120.
Tel: 872 3501 (home)
        964 8400 (work)

TR Register Australia - ACT,
Contact: Graham Brohan,
71 Solomon Cr.,
Latham,
ACT 2615.
Tel: 254 7875

TR Register Australia - Queensland,
Contact: Geoff Fast,
6 Raglass Street,
Everton Park,
Queensland 4053.
Tel: 355 0971

TR Register Australia - South Australia,
Contact: Geoff Bills,
9/195 North Terrace,
Adelaide,
South Australia 5000.
Tel: 332 7561

TR Register Australia - Tasmania,
Contact: Mike Sullivan,
29 Murray Street,
Evan Dale,
Tasmania 7212.
Tel: 91 8223

TR Register - Victoria,
Contact: Graeme White,
13 Malcolm Court,
Ringwood East,
Victoria 3155.
Tel: 870 2782

TR Register - Western Australia,
Contact: Bill Parker,
Box 175,
North Perth,
Western Australia 6006.
Tel: 328 3804

Triumph Sports Owners Association of NSW,
Contact: Bruce Meppem,
9 Bancroft Avenue,
Roseville,
NSW 2069.

Triumph Sports Owners Association of Queensland,
Contact: Paul Bingham,
14 Koolewong Parade,
Ashmore,
Queensland 4214.
Tel: 391070

Triumph Sports Owners Association SA Inc.,
PO Box 192,
Glenside,
South Australia 5065.

Triumph Sports Owners Association (Victoria Inc),
PO Box 5020Y,
Melbourne,
Victoria 3001.

Triumph Sports Owners Association of WA.,
Contact: Andy Hamilton,
Box 257,
Nedlands,
Western Australia 6009.
Tel: 310 1083

Austria
English Sports Car Club,
Postfach 413,
A-1171 Vienna.

Belgium
British Car Club ABSL,
Rue du College,
BP 153,
B-4800 Verviers.
Tel/fax: 87 335122

TR Drivers Club,
Contact: Laurence Collins,
Appt 4,
Rue du Vieux Moulin,
B-6780 Turpiange.

Triumph Enthusiast Club Belgium,
Contact: Willy Delzongle,
36 Fazantenlaan,
B-8200 Brugge.

TR Register Belgium
Contact: Francois van Hoof,
Hoogboomsteenweg 83,
2950 Kapellen.
Tel: 6654229

Canada
British Car Council,
Contact: Kim Chevalier,
Bayview Village,
PO Box 91135,
Willowdale,
Ontario M2K 2Y6.

Club Automobile Triumph Canada Inc.,
Contact: Dave Geller,
CP 871,
Pointe Claire - Dorval,
Quebec H9R 4Z6.
Tel: 514 744 4328

Ontario Triumph Club,
414-2 Cadbury Court,
Waterloo,
Ontario N2K 3G4.

Ottawa Valley Triumph Club,
Contact: Dave Huddleson,
5053 Limebank Road,
Manotick,
Ontario K4M 1B2.

Toronto Triumph Club,

PO Box 39,
Don Mills,
Ontario M3C 2R6.
Tel: 416 693 8983

Denmark
Dansk Triumph Automilklub,
Contact: Jens Konrad,
Parkvaenget 6,
DK-8600 Silkeborg.
Tel: 86 82 3151

TR Club Denmark
Contact: Mogens Fischer,
Gammel Avej 4,
DK-3500 Vaerlose.
Tel: 44 44 1906

Finland
Triumph Cars Club of Finland,
Contact: Pasi J. Lehtinen,
Krootilantie 20,
FIN-27510 Eura.
Tel: 38 86 50 299
Fax: 38 82 36 308

France
Nord Triumph Club,
Contact: Jean Christophe Rigault,
18 rue Maurice Thorez,
59990 Estreux.
Tel: 27 36 52 19

Triumph Club de France,
Contact: Marc Baudier,
29 Allee du Forgeron,
78310 Coignieres.
Tel: 34 61 79 03

TR Register France,
Etienne Prothery,
38 rue Breileau,
75016 Paris.
Tel: 45 53 44 64

Germany
TR Drivers Club,
Contact: Claus von Essen,
Barmstedterstrasse 9d,
D-24568 Kaltenkirchen.

TR Register Deutschland E.V.,
Contact: Rolph Molder,
Im Barm 5,
D-30916 Isernhagen.
Tel: 51 3989 4076
Fax: 51 3989 4077

Triumph IG-Sudwest Germany,
Contact: Arthur Williams,
Pletschweg 7,
D-56154 Boppard.
Tel: 6742 81586

Fax: 5742 81560

Holland
TR Club Holland,
Contact: Willem van de Mast,
Hanenburglaan 76,
NL-2565 GW Den Haag.
Tel: 70 3634713

TR Drivers Club,
Contact: Kees Kappetijn,
Pijperlaan 40,
NL-3335 XH Zwindrecht.
Tel: 78 101825

Hong Kong
TR Register Hong Kong,
Contact: Alan Robinson,
301 Asian House,
1 Hennessy Road,
Wanchai.
Tel: 852 866 3688
Fax: 852 529 5056

Ireland
TR Register Ireland,
Contact: Patrick McMahon,
7 Bellevue Heights,
Greystone,
Co. Wicklow.
Tel: 2876449

Italy
TR Driver Club,
Contact: Nick Lyle,
Via Della Chiesa 10/5,
22060 Sirtori (co).
Tel: 39 9211360

TR Register Italy,
Via Amendola No. 5,
Cernusco Sul Naviglio,
(MI) 20063.
Tel: 29 2105688
Fax: 29 2105460

Japan
TR Register of Japan,
Contact: Susumu Osada,
10-88 Imazudezaike-cho,
Nishinomua City,
Hyogo-Pref 663.

New Zealand
Auckland Triumph Club,
Contact: Basil Lawrence,
Unit 1,
178 Church Street,
Onehunga,
Auckland.
Tel: 9 636 8311 (home)

TR Register of New Zealand,
Contact: Julie Peet
PO Box 17-138,
Greenlane,
Auckland.
Tel: 9 520 3618

Norway
TR Register Norway,
Contact: David Adams,
Hissingbydalen,
1640 Rade.
Tel: 69 284391
Fax: 69 285385

Portugal
Triumph TR Club Portugal,
Contact: Luis M. S. Zoio,
Urb. Portela,
Lt-142, 6 Dto,
2685 Sacavem.

South Africa
Border Triumph Sports Car Club,
Contact: Gavin Turner,
4 Bamburgh Road,
Stirling,
East London 5241.

Pretoria Triumph Sports Car Club,
Contact: Chris Gibbons,
PO Box 1742,
Halfway House,
1685 Pretoria.

Triumph Sports Car Club of Natal,
Contact: Graham Cheetham,
PO Box 29252,
Maydon Wharf 4057.
Tel: 31 764 0938

Triumph Sports Car Club of South Africa,
(Bloemfontein Centre),
Contact: Deon De Kock,
3 Kriek Street,
Fichardt Park,
Bloemfontein 9301.
Tel: 51 22 4328

Triumph Sports Car Club of South Africa,
(Cape Town Centre),
Contact: Dave Gordon,
PO Box 2635,
Cape Town 8000.
Tel: 21 52 3468

Triumph Sports Car Club of South Africa,
(Port Elizabeth Centre),
Contact: Chris Manners,
20 Montagne Street,
Woodlands,
Port Elizabeth 6070.

Tel: 41 32 2054

Triumph Sports Car Club of South Africa,
(Johannesburg Centre),
Conact: Des Burton,
PO Box 95,
Bassonia 2061
Tel: 11 432 2625

Spain
Club TR Register Espana,
Contact: Jacques Parser,
Estrellas 14,
28224 Pozuelo de Alarcon,
Madrid.

Sweden
Triumph TR Club Sweden,
Contact: Eva Eklund,
Trakarrslattsv. 48B,
S-427 51 Billdal.
Tel: 31 277077
Fax: 31 874004

Switzerland
Swiss TR Club,
Heinz Beanz-Baur,
Grubenstr 29,
CH6315 Oberageri/ZG.
Tel: 42 72 06 32
Fax: 42 72 08 32

UK
Club Triumph,
86 Waggon Road,
Hadley Wood,
Herts. EN4 8BR.
Tel: 0181 440 9000
Fax: 0181 440 4694

Club Triumph (Eastern),
Membership Secretary: Peter Condon,
193 Mawney Road,
Romford,
Essex RM7 8BX.
Tel: 01708 705365

TR Drivers Club,
Membership Secretary: Jeff Black,
3 Blackberry Close,
Abbeymead,
Gloucester, GL4 7BS.
Tel: 01452 613590

TR Register,
1B Hawksworth,
Southmead Industrial Park,
Didcot,
Oxon OX11 7HR.
Tel: 01235 818866
Fax: 01235 818867

Triumph TR Club,
Honorary Secretary: Gordon Exell,
'Sheldon',
Smithy Lane,
Willaston,
South Wirral, L64 2UB.
Tel: 0151 327 5174

USA
Capital Florida Triumph Register (TROA),
Contact: Bill Wilkinson,
1701 Grange Circle,
Longwood,
Florida 32750.
Tel: 407 260 5587

Capital Triumph Register,
Contact: Charlie Brown,
2400 Stone Hedge Drive,
Alexandria,
Virginia 22306.
Tel: 703 768 6295

Central Illinois Triumph Owners Association,
Contact: Greg Petrolati,
4014 Danbury Drive,
Champaign,
Illinois 61821.

Central Ohio Center (TROA),
Contact: Susie Householder,
804 N. High Street,
Lancaster,
Ohio 43130
Tel: 614 653 1686.

Central Pennsylvanian Triumph Club,
Contact: Dick James,
23 Houston Drive,
Mechanicsburg,
Pennsylvania 17055.

Connecticut Triumph Register,
Contact: Paul des Rosiers,
Wagon Wheel Lane,
Portland,
Connecticut 06480.
Tel: 203 342 4602

Delaware Valley Triumphs (TROA),
Contact: John Gossin,
525 S. Orange Street,
Media,
Pennsylvania 19063
Tel: 215 565 6432.

Detroit Triumph Sportscar Club,
Contact: Herb J. Hummer,
13201 Common Road,
Warren,
Michigan 48093.
Tel: 313 574 9394

Hawkeye Triumphs,
Contact: Brian Fanton,
355 Daws Road,
Hiawatha,
Iowa 52233.

Indiana Triumph Cars,
7510 Allisonville Road,
Indianapolis,
Indiana 46250.
Tel: 317 841 7677

Kansas City Triumphs,
Contact: Ted Honig,
7605 Johnson Drive,
Shawnee Mission,
Kansas 66202.

Mason-Dixon Triumphs (TROA),
Contact: Marty Jones,
5700 Lakeside Drive,
Sykesville,
Maryland 21784
Tel: 301 795 0177.

Miami Valley Triumphs (TROA),
Contact: Bruce Clough,
PO Box 292824,
Kettering,
Ohio 45429.
Tel: 513 294 3792

Michigan Triumph Association (TROA),
Contact: Joseph Germay,
9349 S. Westnedge,
Kalamazoo,
Michigan 49002
Tel: 616 327 9262.

Minnesota Triumphs,
Contact: Peter Kienzle,
PO Box 201054,
Bloomington,
Minnesota 55420.
Tel: 612 890 5049

New England Triumphs (TROA),
Contact: Bob Groves,
46 Rollingwood,
Elliot,
Maine 03908.
Tel: 207 439 3038

New Jersey Triumph Association,
Contact: Buzz Anthony,
PO Box 6,
Gillette,
New Jersey 07933.
Tel: 908 906 5659

137

North Coast Triumph Association (TROA),
Contact: Bruce Lapiere,
42 Aaron Street,
Berea,
Ohio 44017.
Tel: 216 650 9487

Portland Triumph Owners Association,
PO Box 14105,
Portland,
Oregon 97214.
Tel: 503 246 6687

Rocky Mountain Triumph Club,
Contact: Glenn Sorensen,
PO Box 300426,
Denver,
Colorado 80203-0426.
Tel: 303 220 9742

St Louis Triumph Association,
Contact: David Massey,
321 Peek Kirkwood,
Missouri 63122.

Texas Triumph Register (TROA),
Contact: Mike Hado,
8319 Partlow Lane,
Houston,
Texas 77040.
Tel: 713 937 9042

The Six Pack,
Contact: Beverley Floyd,
1617 Harmony Road,
Akron,
Ohio 44333.

Triumph Club of the Carolinas (TROA),
Contact: Jim Tillman,
Route 4,
Box 472-A,
Charlotte,
North Carolina 28205.

TR Drivers Club,
Contact: Eric Shoaf,
10 Hilton Avenue,
Rhode Island 02915.
Tel: 401 437 2247

Triumph Register of America,
Contact: Ron Hartley,
Suite TR3,
1641 N. Memorial Drive,
Lancaster,
Ohio 43130
Tel: 614 756 4575

Triumph Register of Southern California (TROA),
Contact: Bob Youngdahl,
10328 Jovita Avenue,
Chatsworth,
California 92138.
Tel: 818 718 1426

Triumph Sports Car Club of San Diego,
PO Box 84342,
San Diego,
California 92138.
Tel: 619 484 6114

Triumph Standard Motor Club of Florida,
Contact: Jack Russell,
11302 Regal Lane,
Largo,
Florida 34644.
Tel: 813 446 2478

Triumph Travellers Sports Car Club (TROA),
Contact: Teriann Wakeman,
725 Trout Gulch Road,
Aptos,
California 95003.
Tel: 415 857 5057

Vintage Triumphs of Wisconsin,
Contact: Chuck Salamun,
1505 4th Avenue,
Grafton,
Wisconsin 53024.

Vintage Triumph Register,
15218 West Warren Avenue,
Dearborn,
Michigan 48126.

APPENDIX II

PAINT & TRIM CODES

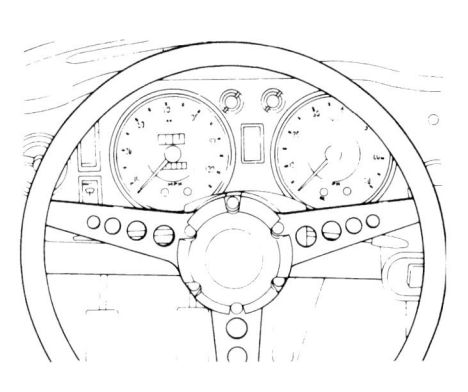

Basic colour codes

A TR6's original basic colour is identified by the final number in the paint code which can be found on the commission plate that is either fixed to the nearside inner front wing, or on the nearside 'B' post on later cars. "96," for example, is Sapphire Blue; "6" being blue and "9" the shade. Triumph used a system comprising nine basic colours allocated number codes as follows -

1	Black
2	Red
3	Brown
4	Yellow
5	Green
6	Blue
7	Purple
8	Grey
9	White

Trim codes

11	Black
12	Matador Red
13	Light Tan
27	Shadow Blue
33	New Tan
63	Chestnut
74	Beige

1968 model year colours

12	Matador Red
32	Signal Red
34	Jasmine Yellow
25	Triumph Racing Green/Conifer
26	Wedgwood Blue
56	Royal Blue
19	White

1969 model year colours

12	Matador Red
32	Signal Red
34	Jasmine Yellow
25	Triumph Racing Green/Conifer
55	Laurel Green
56	Royal Blue
17	Damson
27	Shadow Blue
19	White

1970 model year colours

12	Matador Red
32	Signal Red
34	Jasmine Yellow
25	Triumph Racing Green/Conifer
55	Laurel Green
56	Royal Blue
17	Damson
27	Shadow Blue
19	White

1971 model year colours

32	Signal Red
23	Sienna Brown
34	Jasmine Yellow
54	Saffron Yellow
55	Laurel Green
56	Royal Blue
17	Damson
19	White

1972 model year colours

72	Pimento Red
23	Sienna Brown
34	Jasmine Yellow
54	Saffron Yellow
65	Emerald Green
96	Sapphire Blue
17	Damson
19	White

139

1973 model year colours
72 .... Pimento Red
82 .... Carmine Red
92 .... Magenta
23 .... Sienna Brown
64 .... Mimosa Yellow
65 .... Emerald Green
96 .... Sapphire Blue
106 .... Mallard Blue
126 .... French Blue
19 .... White

1974 model year colours
72 .... Pimento Red
82 .... Carmine Red
92 .... Magenta
83 .... Maple
64 .... Mimosa Yellow
65 .... Emerald Green
96 .... Sapphire Blue
106 .... Mallard Blue
126 .... French Blue
19 .... White

1975 model year colours
72 .... Pimento Red
82 .... Carmine Red
83 .... Maple
64 .... Mimosa Yellow
84 .... Topaz Yellow
75 .... British Racing Green
85 .... Java Green
126 .... French Blue
136 .... Delft Blue
19 .... New White

1976 model year colours
72 .... Pimento Red
82 .... Carmine Red
93 .... Russet Brown
64 .... Mimosa Yellow
84 .... Topaz Yellow
94 .... Inca Yellow
65 .... Tahiti Blue
75 .... British Racing Green
85 .... Java Green
126 .... French Blue
136 .... Delft Blue
19 .... New White

Paint colour and trim combinations

The variety of colours available on the TR6 was as follows:

Paint colour	Years	Matching trim (years offered in brackets)
17 Damson	1968-72	Black (68-72), Light Tan 68/69), New Tan (69-72)
19 New White	1968-76	Black (68-76), Matador Red (68-72), Light Tan (68/69), New Tan (70-72), Shadow Blue (71-75), Chestnut (72-76), Beige (76)
23 Siena Brown	1969-73	Black (69-73), New Tan (69-73)
25 Triumph Racing Green (aka Conifer Green)	1968-69	Black, Light Tan and, possibly, Matador Red
26 Wedgwood Blue	1968	Black and Light Tan
32 Signal Red	1968-71	Black (68-71), Light Tan (68/69), New Tan (69-71)
34 Jasmine Yellow	1968-72	Black (68-71), Light Tan (68/69), New Tan (69-72)
54 Saffron Yellow	1970-72	Black and New Tan
55 Laurel Green	1969-72	Black (69-72), New Tan (69-71), Matador Red (1969/70)
56 Royal Blue	1968-71	Black and Shadow Blue
64 Mimosa Yellow	1972-76	Black (72-76), Chestnut (72-76), Beige (75/76)
65 Emerald Green	1971-74	Black
72 Pimento Red	1971-76	Black (71-76), Chestnut (72-76)
73 Maple Beige	1973-76	Black (73-76), New Tan (73/74), Beige (75/76)
75 British Racing Green	1974-76	Black (74-76), Beige (75/76)
82 Carmine Red	1972-76	Black (72-75), New Tan (72-74), Beige 75/76)
83 Maple	1973-76	Black (73-75), New Tan (73/74), Beige (75/76)
84 Topaz Yellow	1974-76	Black (74-76), Beige (75/76)
85 Java Green	1974-76	Black
92 Magenta	1972-74	Black
93 Russet Brown	1976	Beige
94 Inca Yellow	1976	Black
96 Sapphire Blue	1971-74	Black and Shadow Blue
106 Mallard Blue	1972-74	Black and New Tan
126 French Blue	1972-76	Black
136 Delft Blue	1974-76	Black (74-76), Shadow Blue (74/75)
146 Tahiti Blue	1976	Black and Beige

APPENDIX III

TR6 TECHNICAL SPECIFICATIONS & GENERAL DATA

Injection cars: Nov 1968-Sept: 1972 CP series built
                      Nov 1972-Jan 1975 CR series built
Carburettor cars: Sept 1968-Oct 1972 CC series built
                      Sept 1972-Jul 1976 CF series built

Engine

Number of cylinders 6
Bore of cylinders .... 74.7mm/2.94 inches
Stroke of crank .... 95.0mm/3.74 inches
Capacity .... 2498cc/152 cubic inches
Max power .... 150bhp (SAE) at 5500rpm (CP series)
                               124bhp (DIN) at 5000rpm (CR series)
                               111bhp (SAE) at 4500rpm ('68 CC series)
                               104bhp (SAE) at 4500rpm ('69-'71 CC series)
                               106bhp (SAE) at 4900rpm ('72-'73 CC and CF)
                               101bhp (DIN) at 4900rpm ('74-'76 CF series)
Max torque .... 164lb/ft (SAE) at 3500rpm (CP series)
                               143lb/ft (DIN) at 3500rpm (CR series)
                               152lb/ft (SAE) at 3000rpm ('68 CC series)
                               142lb/ft (SAE) at 3000rpm ('69-'71 CC series)
                               133lb/ft (SAE) at 3000rpm ('72-'73 CC and CF)
                               128lb/ft (DIN) at 3000rpm ('74-'76 CF series)
Compression ratio .... Injection: 9.5:1
                               Carbs '68-71: 8.5:1,
                               1972 & 1973: 7.75:1.
                               1974 on: 7.5:1
Firing order 1, 5, 3, 6, 2, 4
Cylinder block .... Chrome cast iron.
Cylinder head .... Chrome cast iron.
Pistons .... Aluminium alloy.
Connecting rods .... 60 ton steel with floating gudgeon pins.
Crankshaft .... Robust construction with integral balance weights.
Bearings .... 4 main bearings. Aluminium tin.
Valves .... Pushrod operated overhead valves.
Camshaft .... Five bearings, hyposine cams, chain driven.
Cooling system .... No loss system.
Circulation .... Pump driven by V-belt. Thermostatically controlled flow.
Fan .... Pre-1971: 8 blades, 12.5 inches diameter.
                               1971/72: 7 blades, 12.5 inches diameter.
                               1973 on: 13 blades, 14.5 inches diameter.

Manifolds	....	3 twin inlet manifolds, with 6 throttle valves on injection cars. A '2 into 6' one-piece inlet manifold, water-heated by a pipe from the water pump on the carburettored cars. Twin outlet exhaust manifold.
Air cleaner	....	Replaceable paper element type.
Lubrication	....	Oil pump - high capacity, submerged, eccentric lobe type. Feed to main bearings, big ends and all camshaft bearings under pressure.
Warning lamp	....	Extinguishes at 3-5lb/sq.in.
Oil filter	....	Full-flow type with replaceable element.
Generator	....	Lucas 15ACR alternator, output 28 amps.
Engine mountings	....	Flexible rubber mountings for engine and gearbox unit.
Exhaust system	....	Twin pipe system flexibly mounted and insulated against noise transmission to the body.
Crankcase	....	Closed circuit breathing system through one valve to inlet manifold.
Flywheel	....	Cast iron with hardened steel starter ring gear.
Ignition coil	....	Pre-1973: Lucas HA12. 1973 onwards: Lucas 15c6 (used with ballast resistor).
Ignition timing	....	11 degrees b.t.d.c.
Distributor	....	Lucas 22-6.
Contact breaker gap	......	0.0015in
Spark plugs	....	N9Y set at 0.0025in.

Fuel system

Type	....	Tank at rear, electric lift pump, Lucas fuel injection on CP and CR series cars. Twin Stromberg 1.75 CD 2SE on US bound CC series cars. Superseded in 1972 by 175 CD-SEVs on US bound CF series cars.

Transmission

Clutch	....	Diaphragm type 8.5in diameter hydraulically operated.
Gearbox	....	Four forward ratios with synchromesh and reverse.
Overdrive when fitted	....	All CP commission series and cars up to CR567 - Laycock 'A' type overdrive unit operating on 2nd, 3rd and top gears. Ratio 0.82: 1. Cars from commission number CR567 - Laycock 'J' unit on 3rd and top gears. Ratio 0.797: 1.

Ratios
Cars up to gearbox CD51163

	O'drive Top	Top	O'drive 3rd	3rd	O'drive 2nd	2nd	1st	Rev
Ratios	0.82	1.00	1.09	1.33	1.65	2.01	3.14	3.22
Overall ratios	2.83	3.45	3.76	4.59	5.69	6.94	10.83	11.11

Cars from gearbox CD51164 onwards

	O'drive Top 'J'	O'drive Top 'A'	Top	O'drive 3rd 'J'	O'drive 3rd 'A'	3rd	O'drive 2nd 'A' only	2nd	1st	Rev
Ratios	0.797	0.82	1.00	1.11	1.10	1.39	1.66	2.10	2.99	3.37
Overall ratios	2.75	2.83	3.45	3.83	3.76	4.78	5.69	7.25	10.33	11.62

Prop shaft	....	All metal shaft, needle roller bearings.
Rear axle	....	Final drive unit rubber mounted. Hypoid bevel gears. Taper roller bearings. Ratio 3.45: 1.

Suspension

Front .... Low periodicity independent system.
Patented bottom bush and top ball joint swivels.
Coil springs controlled by telescopic dampers.
Taper roller hub bearings.
Anti-roll bar 5/8in diameter steel bar.

Rear .... Semi-trailing arm independent suspension with coil springs controlled by piston dampers.
Trailing arms mounted to chassis through rubber bushed pivots.
Springs also mounted on rubber pads.

Wheels

Type .... Steel wheels 5.5J section, 15in diameter.
Centre trims .... 1969 cars: simulated magnesium trim as on TR5.
1970-73: small black plastic centres bearing TR6 logo.
1973 on: centres silver with TR6 logo.
Wires .... Wire wheels optional until CR series. 51/2K section 15in diameter, 72 spoke centre lock, finished in silver.

Tyres

Sizes .... Dunlop 165HR - 15 SP Sport Michelin 165 HR - 15 XAS.

Brakes

Front .... Caliper disc brakes.
Total swept area 233 sq.in.
10.9in diameter
Rear .... Drum brakes. 9 x 1.75in of leading and trailing shoe-type on rear wheels. Total swept area 99 sq. in.
Pedal operates through direct acting servo and tandem master cylinder in front and rear brakes independently.
Handbrake .... Mechanical on rear wheels only.

Frame (chassis)

Type .... Rigid structure, channel steel pressings form box section side members, braced by cruciform member.

Steering

Type .... Rack and pinion type with energy-absorbing steering column system. 3.25 turns lock-to-lock.
Steering wheel .... 1969 model: leather rim, black spokes, 15in diameter.
1970-73: leather rim, anodised slotted spokes, 15in diameter.
1973 on: leather rim, anodised slotted spokes, 14.5in diameter.

Battery

Type .... 12 volt, 57 amp hour, located under the bonnet.
Polarity .... Negative earth system.

External dimensions

Length 3937mm/12ft 11in
Width 1470mm/4ft 10in
Wheelbase 2240mm/7ft 4in

Track front 1276mm/4ft 2.25in
Track rear 1264mm/4ft 1.75in
Height (unladen)............ 1270mm/4ft 2in
Ground clearance 152mm/6in
Turning circle
   up to 1971 .... 10.1 metres/33ft
   1971 onwards 10.4 metres/34ft

Interior dimensions
Seat width (each) 483mm/19in
Seating width
   (between doors) 1232mm/48.5in
Seat height
   (from floor) 222mm/8.75in
Seat depth
   (fore and aft) 457mm/18in
Headroom
   (from seat cushion)... 864mm/34in
Steering wheel clearance
   from cushion 140mm/5.5in
Steering wheel clearance
   from seat squab .... Min   381mm/15in
                                  Max 483mm/19in
Seat squab to
   clutch pedal .... Min   914mm/36in
                                  Max 1016mm/40in
Width of door opening
   at waist 720mm/28in
Interior width
   between sills............. 1230mm/48.75in

Maximum interior
   height 1030mm/40.5in

Luggage space
Behind the seats
   length .... Min   380mm/15in
                                Max 483mm/19in
Width between
   rear wheelarches 845mm/33.4in
Height, front (floor
   to top of seats) 535mm/21in
Boot capacity .... 16 cu. metres/5.6 cu.ft
Boot height .... Min   190mm/7.5in
                                  Max 304mm/13.5in
Boot depth
   (fore and aft) 520mm/20.5in
Boot width.................... 1140mm/45in
Boot opening width .... Min   980mm/38.5in
                                  Max 1015mm/40in

Weight
Dry (excluding extra
   equipment) 1053kg/20.75cwt
Basic kerb (inc. water,
   fuel, oil and tools) 1085kg/21.50cwt
Gross vehicle weight
   pre '71 .... 1308kg/25.75cwt
Gross vehicle weight
   1971 model on 1360kg/26.75cwt

Body & interior
Type .... 2-seater convertible sports, available with removable hard top. All steel body. Detachable windscreen with toughened safety glass. Doors hinged at front. Front and rear wings bolted on.

Seating .... 2 bucket-type seats, adjustable fore and aft. Both seats pivot forward to allow access to rear shelf and are retained by quick release self-locking type catches. Seats reclined from 1970 on. Head restraints available on CR cars as an optional extra.

Upholstery .... PVC leathercloth. 'Ambla' ventilated seat facings.

Instruments .... 5in tachometer and 5in speedometer with trip meter positioned in front of driver. Separate gauges for fuel, water temperature, oil pressure and ammeter. (CR cars had voltmeter in place of ammeter). Ingition and oil warning light incorporated in tachometer. High beam and trafficator warning lamp incorporated in speedometer. CP series cars blue lighting to instruments. CR series cars green lighting to instruments. Rheostat control for instrument lights in facia centre.

Controls .... Ignition: '69 cars, as TR5 with ignition lock positioned in centre control binacle to left of choke. 1970 on: combined ignition and steering lock positioned directly below column under lower crashpad. Lock padded for driver crash protection.

Switch types for
   accessories .... Knobs for choke, heater, fan and air distribution. Rocker switches for 2-speed wipers and washers. (Revised on the CR series).

| | Cars to 1973: column switches for indicators and overdrive plus 3-position lighting switch (off, sidelights and dipped headlamps) plus daylight flash facility. Foot-operated dipswitch.
Cars from 1973: column switches for overdrive, indicators and lighting dipswitch. Lighting control now on dashboard replacing wiper switch. |
|---|---|
| Luggage | Glovebox on dashboard, map pockets in doors. Luggage space behind seats and in boot. |
| Petrol tank | Mounted between rear wheelarches with filler cap mounted centrally in rear deck panel. |

General equipment

| Interior | Interior dipping mirror with breakaway support.
Padded swivelling sun visors with vanity mirror on passenger side.
Satin wood finish dashboard with padded surround incorporating a shielded control panel for occupant safety.
Ashtray fitted on top of facia.
Padded door waist rails. Safety belts. Carpets with thick felt underlay.
Interior lamp.
Boot lamp. |
|---|---|
| Heating & ventilation | Heater with 2-speed blower, providing air of the required temperature to the car's interior and which incorporates a demisting facility.
Face-level ventilation provided by 2 eyeball vents at either end of the dashboard.
Foot-level ventilation provided by eyeball vents under facia. |
| Exterior | Headlamps to suit market requirements.
Front indicators and sidelights mounted below grille.
Repeater lamps for direction indicators mounted on front wing ahead of wheelarch.
Rear side/stop lights, reversing lights and indicators plus wrap-round body onto rear wing housing repeater lamps for direction indicators.
Number plate illumination: CP series cars - 2 lamps on bumper in separate housing; CR series cars - 2 lamps fitted into bodywork above number plate.
Electric windscreen washers.
Twin windtone horns concealed behind front valance.
PVC soft top incorporates rear window and quarter-lights. Rear window zips out. Hood fitted with concealed safety catches above header rail.
Front hinged bonnet released from nearside footwell.
Safety catch plus prop.
One-piece chrome-plated front bumper, three-piece chrome-plated rear bumper.
Self-parking 2-speed wipers.
Spare wheel and tyre, wheelbrace, jack and toolroll. |

Capacities

Fuel tank	
up to 1973	51 litres/11.25 Imperial gallons
1973 onwards	48.6 litres/10.75 Imperial gallons
Engine sump	4.25 litres/8 pints
Gearbox from dry	1.13 litres/2 pints
Gearbox and overdrive from dry	
'A' type	2.0 litres/3.5 pints
'J' type	1.5 litres/2.66 pints
Rear axle from dry	
up to 1970	1.42 litres/2.5 pints
1970 onwards	1.27 litres/2.25 pints
Cooling system	6.2 litres/11 pints

Engine/road speeds
Cars fitted with gearbox number up to CD51162

	Top	3rd	2nd	1st
Engine speed at 10mph	471	626	947	1479
Engine speed at 10kph	292	393	595	940

Cars fitted with gearbox number CD51163 onwards

	Top	3rd	2nd	1st
Engine speed at 10mph	471	654	990	1412
Engine speed at 10kph	292	406	621	878

Road speed at
1000rpm in top gear 21.21mph/34.2kph
Road speed at
2500ft/min piston
speed in top gear 85mph/137kph

Maximum recommended speeds in intermediate gears (as taken from the Triumph sales catalogue)
1969 CP series cars fitted with gearbox number up to CD51162
1st 37mph/60kph
2nd 58mph/93kph
3rd 88mph/142kph

1974 CR series cars fitted with gearbox number CD51163 onwards
1st 41mph/66kph
2nd 59mph/94kph
3rd 89mph/143kph

Performance data
These are the figures given in the Triumph TR6 sales brochures of 1969 and 1974 respectively. Figures recorded by contemporary road testers do vary.

	CP Series		CR Series
Max power	150bhp (SAE) at 5500rpm	Max power	124bhp (DIN) at 5000rpm
Max torque	164lb/ft (SAE) at 3500 rpm	Max torque	143lb/ft (DIN) at 3500rpm

Acceleration (through gears)
0-30mph .... Not given .... 3.5 secs
0-50mph .... 6.5 secs .... 7.0 secs
0-60mph .... 9.0 secs .... 9.5 secs

Acceleration (top gear)
30-50mph .... 7.0 secs .... 8.0 secs
40-60mph .... 7.0 secs .... 8.0 secs
50-70mph .... Not given .... 8.5 secs

Acceleration (through gears)
0-40kph .... Not given .... 3.0 secs
0-80kph .... Not given .... 7.0 secs
0-100kph .... Not given .... 9.5 secs

Acceleration (top gear)
50-80kph .... 7.0 secs .... 8.0 secs
70-100kph .... 7.0 secs .... 8.0 secs

Max speed .... 115-125mph 116mph

How the TR6 compares
Comparison is with CP Commission number series TR6

Car	Price	Max speed	0-60mph
TR6 (with o/d)	£1339	117 mph	9.0 secs
MGC	£1330	119 mph	8.6 secs
TVR Vixen S	£1487	109 mph	10.5 secs
Morgan Plus 8	£1507	125 mph	7.0 secs
Reliant Scimitar GT	£1577	120 mph	9.4 secs

Basic routine maintenance/servicing schedule
See owner's handbook for full schedule

Maximum service interval .... 6000 miles

Every 6000 miles .... Change engine oil (8 pints) and filter
                                   Clean oil filter
                                   Lubricate distributor
                                   Clean and check plug gaps
                                   Grease 6 chassis lube points

Every 12,000 miles .... Adjust valve clearances
                                   Change spark plugs
                                   Clean fuel filter and crankcase emission valve
                                   Grease water pump and handbrake
                                   Adjust front hubs and rear brakes

APPENDIX IV

CHASSIS NUMBER SEQUENCES, SIGNIFICANT DATES & SALES QUANTITIES

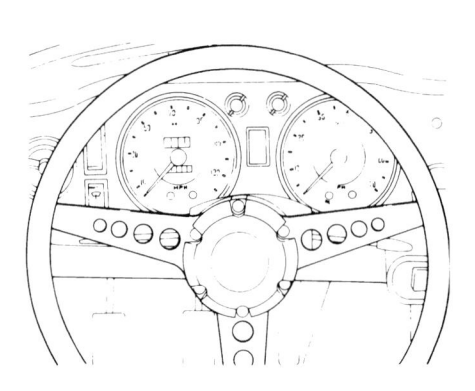

Chassis number sequences

1969*
Petrol Injection	CP25001 Prototype
	CP25002 - CP25145 CKD kits
	CP25146 First car off the assembly line on 28/11/68
	CP26998 Last 1969 model built around 10/9/69
Carburettor	CC25003L First car built on 19/9/68)
	CC32142L Last 1969 model built on 19/12/69

1970-1971*
Petrol Injection	CP50001 First 1970 model built on 1/9/69
	CP50002 - CP50436 CKD kits
	CP54572 Last 1971 model built on 7/9/71
Carburettor	CC50001L First 1970 model built on 22/11/69
	CC67893L Last 1971 model built on 20/8/71

1972*
Petrol Injection	CP75001 First 1972 model built on 27/9/71
	CP77718 Last 1972 model built on 21/9/72
Carburettor	CC75001L First 1972 model built on 20/8/71
	CC85737U Last 1972 model built on 5/10/72

1973*
Petrol Injection	CR169 First 1973 model built on 15/11/72
	CR1 - CR168 CKD kits
	CR2911 Last 1973 model built on 17/10/73
Carburettor	CF1U First 1973 model built on 11/9/72

1974*
Petrol Injection	CR5049 First 1974 model built on 14/9/73
	CR5001 - CR5048 CKD kits
Carburettor	CF25777U Last 1974 model built on 18/9/74

1975*
Petrol Injection	CR6701 Last injection car built on 7/2/75
Carburettor	CF27002U First 1975 model built on 22/8/74
	CF39991U Last 1975 model built on 23/8/75

1976*
Carburettor	CF50001U First 1976 model built on 29/8/75
	CF58328U Last TR6 built on 15/7/76

Significant dates

Date	Chassis number	Comment
19/9/68	CC25003L	First TR6 built
28/11/68	CP25146	First injection car built
1/9/69	CP50001	First 1970 injection model built
10/9/69	CP26998	Last 1969 injection model believed built
22/11/69	CC50001L	First 1970 carburettor model built
19/12/69	CC32142L	Last 1969 carburettor model built
20/8/71	CC67893L	Last 1971 carburettor model built
20/8/71	CC75001L	First 1972 carburettor model built
7/9/71	CP54572	Last 1971 injection model built
27/9/71	CP75001	First 1972 injection model built
11/9/72	CF1U	First 1973 carburettor model built
21/9/72	CP77718	Last 1972 injection model built
5/10/72	CC85737U	Last 1972 carburettor built
15/11/72	CR 169	First 1973 injection model built
14/9/73	CR5049	First 1974 injection model built
17/10/73	CR2911	Last 1973 injection model built
22/8/74	CF27002U	First 1975 carburettor model
18/9/74	CF25777U	Last 1974 carburettor model built
7/2/75	CR6701	Last injection car built
23/8/75	CF39991U	Last 1975 carburettor model built
29/8/75	CF50001U	First 1976 carburettor model built
15/7/76	CF58328	Last TR6 made

Sales quantities

Home market
Year	Quantity
1968	0
1969	704
1970	1308
1971	1288
1972	1720
1973	1948
1974	843
1975	545
1976	14

Total (home market) 8370

Export
Year	Quantity
1968	1519
1969	7981
1970	10795
1971	12203
1972	11724
1973	11705
1974	13740
1975	9228
1976	7208
1977	146

Total (export) 86249

TOTAL SALES (ALL MARKETS) 94619

* Model years, cars not necessarily built in that year.

APPENDIX V

COX & BUCKLES TR REGISTER RACE CHAMPIONSHIP REGULATIONS

These regulations are reproduced here in abridged form as the point of their inclusion is simply to give an idea of what needs to be done to a TR6 to make it suitable for motor racing. For example, Class A is for roadgoing cars where the modifications are limited to safety items, while Class E is for out and out racing cars where numerous modifications are allowed.

If you wish to race in this series contact the TR Register to ensure you receive the latest set of regulations.

Competitor eligibility

Entrants must be fully paid-up valid membership card-holding members of the TR Register and in possession of a valid RACMSA Entrants Licence or equivalent EC licence.

Drivers and Entrant/Drivers must be fully paid-up valid membership card-holding members of the TR Register, be registered for the Championship and in possession of a valid RACMSA Competition (Racing) National B Status Licence or equivalent EC licence.

All documentation must be presented for checking at all rounds when signing on.

Registration

All drivers must register as competitors for the championship by returning the Registration Form with the Registration Fee to the Co-ordinator prior to the final closing date for the first round being entered.

The Registration Fee is £25 per car per class, made payable to the TR Register.

Registrations are acceptable from 1st January until 28th February. Late entered competitors (a) will be given a lower priority than those registered within the time limit for registration in the allocation of entries where races are over-subscribed, (b) will score no points in the Championship, (c) points will be allocated as if the person was not competing, (d) for the purposes of allocating points they will not be included in the number of starters in each class.

Registration numbers will be the permanent Competition numbers for the Championship.

Scoring

Points will be awarded to Competitors listed as classified finishers in the Final Results as follows:
4 or more starters in the class - 1st 8, 2nd 6, 3rd 4, 4th 2.

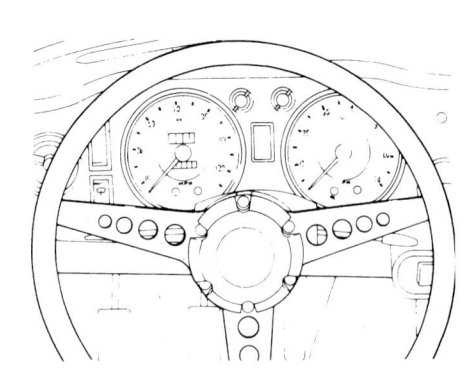

3 starters in the class - 1st 6, 2nd 4, 3rd 2.
2 starters in the class - 1st 4, 2nd 2.
1 starter in the class - 1st 2

One additional point will be awarded to each competitor achieving or equalling the race fastest lap in each class, where the race is timed. One additional point to be awarded to every driver who comes under starter's orders.
Any driver scoring points in more than one class will not be allowed to add his points together for the purpose of determining his standing in the overall Championship.

The totals from all qualifying rounds less 2 will determine final Championship points and positions.

Ties shall be resolved in the following order:
    (a) Greatest number of class wins
    (b) Greatest number of starts over the total number of races
    (c) Greatest number of new class lap records over the season
    (d) Greatest number of competitors beaten in his class over his qualifying rounds

Awards
All awards are to be provided by the TR Register.

Per round: trophies to 1st, 2nd and 3rd in class.

Championship:
    Overall Champion - TR Register Race Championship Trophy and Replica.
    Newcomers Champion - TR Register Race Championship Newcomers Trophy and Replica.
    Trophies to 1st, 2nd and 3rd in class.
    Paul Good Trophy - most original TR2 or 3.
    Chestnut House Trophy - Best prepared private car.
    Perseverance Plate - Chairman's Award.

TECHNICAL REGULATIONS

Introduction
The following Technical Regulations are set out in accordance with the RACMSA specified format and it should be clearly understood that if the following texts do not clearly specify that you can do it, you should work on the principle that you cannot.

General description
The TR Register Championship is for Competitors participating in Triumph TR2-8, Swallow Doretti, Warwick, Dove and Peerless vehicles in the following classes:
    A. Roadsports (ie cars must have an MoT). Excludes Replica TR7 Sprint, TR3 Beta and TR7V8.
    C. Tuned 4 cylinder (includes original and replica TR7 Sprints, TR3 Betas and FIA Appendix K cars).
    D. Tuned 6 and 8 cylinder.
    E. Modified.

TRs not currently eligible even for the Modified class but of significant interest can be considered for entry by the Championship Stewards subject to certain limitations.

Safety requirements
All RACMSA Appendix Q Safety Criteria Regulations apply as relevant.

General Technical Requirements Exceptions
Cars must comply with originality on major components of engine type, gearbox casing and axle/differential casing.

Chassis
As original except localised reinforcement of suspension and differential mountings on safety grounds. No other reinforcement/stiffening or lightening permitted. Anyone considering using a reproduction or re-manufactured chassis should consult the Championship Co-ordinator before acquiring one.

Bodywork

General:
ALL CLASSES .... All body panels to be fixed in place as originally. All internal structures including closing panels are to be in their original location. Hardtops permitted. Hood and frame may be removed, flexible tonneau cover may be fitted.
CLASSES A, C, D .... Internal structure must be steel.
CLASS E .... Internal structure must be metal.
CLASSES A .... (TR2, 3, 3A, 3B only), C (except TR7), D (except TR7V8 - 8), E (except TR7, TR7V8 - 8) may remove windscreens.

Interior:
CLASS A........................ Loose trim may be removed. Original dashboard and instruments must be retained.
CLASSES C, D, E .... Dashboard must be in original location and fitted with original type instruments. All trim may be removed. Passenger seat may be removed.

Exterior:
ALL CLASSES .... Fibreglass or alloy panels may be substituted for all outer original steel panels. Bumpers and overriders may be removed.
CLASS E .... Undertrays allowed.

Silhouette:
ALL CLASSES .... Must conform to original silhouette except SAH bonnets may be fitted to TR4, 4A and 5. Original type spoilers may be fitted to TR6, 7, 7V8 and 8 only.
CLASS E .... Wheelarches can be flared to cover the complete wheel around an arch of 120 degrees.

Ground clearance:
CLASS A........................ 3.5 inch minimum
CLASSES C, D .... 3 inch minimum
CLASS E .... Free

Prohibited modifications
General:
ALL CLASSES .... Removal of inner body panels. Fibreglass inner body panels.

Interior:
CLASS A........................ May not remove passenger seat.

Exterior:
CLASS A........................ Radiator grille may not be removed.
CLASSES A, C, D .... No undertrays allowed.

Silhouette:
CLASSES A, C, D .... No flaring of wheelarches.
ALL CLASSES .... No airdams allowed. No spoilers allowed on TR2 - 5, Swallow Doretti, Warwick, Dove and Peerless vehicles.

Engine
Permitted modifications
CLASS A........................ Maximum bore size:

                                      6 cyl engines and TR7 max 060" overbore
                                      4 cyl engines (except TR7) 89mm pistons/liners permitted
                                      Balancing of components
                                      Camshaft 4 cyl. engines free

CLASS C .... Maximum bore size:
                                      TR2 - 4 91.35mm
                                      TR7 - 94.82mm

CLASS D .... Maximum bore size:
                                      TR5/6 - 76.2mm
                                      TR7V8/8 - 89.67mm

CLASS E .... Maximum capacity 3900cc

CLASSES C, D, E .... Balancing and lightening of components. Type of material for rotating components: pistons, crank, clutch, flywheel, conrods, pulleys, dampers free. Camshaft free.

Prohibited modifications
CLASS A .... Lightening of engine components apart from balancing of components.
                                      Non-standard valves in cylinder head.
                                      Camshaft 6 and 8 cyl. engines must be standard.

CLASSES A, C, D .... No supercharging or turbocharging.

CLASS E .... No turbocharging.

ALL CLASSES .... Must use original block and head. No dry sumping.

Location
ALL CLASSES .... Original location.

Oil/water cooling
ALL CLASSES .... Oil coolers permitted.
                                      Radiators free. Fans may be replaced by electric.

Induction systems
CLASS A .... 4 cyl. engines. Max 1.75" SU/Stromberg or original fuel injection system on TR7.
                                      6 and 8 cyl. engines. Original Petrol Injection or Max 2" SU/Stromberg twin carbs.

CLASS C .... Max 2" SU/Stromberg or original fuel injection system on TR7.

CLASS D .... Original Petrol Injection or Max 2" SU/Stromberg twin carbs.

CLASS E .... Free.

Exhaust systems
ALL CLASSES .... Manifolds free.
                                      Exhaust system must comply with RACMSA Blue Book as per section E 13.17.

Ignition systems
ALL CLASSES .... Free.

Fuel delivery systems
ALL CLASSES .... Free.

Suspensions
Permitted modifications

CLASS A .... Original type adjustable front shock absorbers.
Original type adjustable rear shock absorbers.

CLASSES A, C, D .... Front springs: original type, rate free, length free.
Rear springs: original type, rate free, length free.

CLASSES C, D, E .... Front and rear shock absorbers free.

CLASS E .... Front springs free.
Rear springs: original type, rate free, length free.

ALL CLASSES .... Solid bushes may be fitted. Front and rear anti-roll bars free. Front and rear camber, castor and toe free.

Prohibited modifications
CLASS D .... No adjustable platforms TR7V8 - 8.

Wheelbase track
ALL CLASSES .... Wheelbase as original. Track free but refer to Silhouette requirements.

Transmissions
Permitted modifications
CLASSES A, C, D .... Rear axle location. One addition to original.

CLASS E .... Rear axle location free. LSD free.

ALL CLASSES .... Competition type clutch may be fitted.

Prohibited modifications
CLASSES A, C, D .... No Limited Slip or Torque Bias Diffs.

ALL CLASSES .... Non-original gearbox, overdrive, differential and rear axle casing, except TR2 which may use TR3A rear axle.

Transmission and drive ratios
CLASSES A, C, D .... Must use original gearbox ratios except TR7/8 which may use 5-speed gearbox.

CLASS E .... Gearbox ratios free but no 5-speed gearbox except TR7/8.

CLASS A .... TR2-4 may use 3.7 or 4.1 axle ratio.
TR5-6PI cars may use 3.45 axle ratio only.
Carb cars may use 3.45 or 3.7 axle ratio.
TR7-8 may use 3.63 or 3.9 axle ratio.

CLASSES C, D, E .... Rear axle ratios free.

Electrics
Exterior lighting
ALL CLASSES .... Headlamps must be fitted.
Rear lamps must be fitted and brake lights must work.

Rear fog light
ALL CLASSES .... As per RACMSA Section Q5

Batteries
ALL CLASSES .... Must be fitted. Location free.

Generators
CLASSES A, C, D .... Charging system must be operational.

Brakes
Permitted modifications
CLASSES A, C, D .... TR2-6: Brakes may be interchanged. Alfin-type drums permitted.
TR7-8: Brakes may be interchanged.

CLASS E .... Free but all cars must retain standard rear drums.

ALL CLASSES .... Pad and lining material free. Pipes/hoses free. Servo free. Ducting free.

Prohibited modifications
CLASSES A, C, D .... No vented discs.

CLASS E .... No rear discs.

Wheels/steering
Permitted options
ALL CLASSES .... Steering as original but rack may be solid mounted to chassis. Alternative steering wheel allowed.

Construction and materials
ALL CLASSES .... Wire, alloy or steel wheels permitted.

Dimensions
CLASSES A, C, D .... Max rim width 6".

CLASS E .... Max rim width 7".

ALL CLASSES .... TR2-6: 15" rim diameter.
TR7-8: 13" rim diameter.

Tyres
Specifications
CLASSES A, C, D .... Any listed road tyre which has appeared in RACMSA Blue Book section R3.1 inc. Type 1A and 1b. Minimum profile 60%. MoT tyre regulations apply.

CLASS E .... Any treaded road or race tyre. No cut slicks.

Nominated manufacturers
ALL CLASSES .... As above.

Weights
CLASS A	Minimum TR2/3	890kgs
	TR4/SD/Dove/Warwick/Peerless	920kgs
	TR5/6	980kgs
	TR7/7 Sprint	950kgs
	TR8	1095kgs

CLASSES C, D .... Minimum TR2-7 .... 850kgs
TR7V8 - 8... 950kgs

CLASS E .... No minimum weight.

Fuel tank/fuel
Types
ALL CLASSES .... Free.

Locations
CLASS A....................... As original.

CLASSES C, D, E .... Within the luggage compartment.

Fuel
ALL CLASSES .... Pump fuel only allowed as defined by RACMSA.

Silencing
Specification
ALL CLASSES .... All cars must be fitted with silencers which comply with the current RACMSA noise levels as per Section E.13.17 of the Blue Book.

Numbers and Championship decals
Positions
All cars will be required to carry a Championship decal bearing the name of the series sponsor - Cox & Buckles - preferably on the rear of the front wing on either side of the car. Any car not displaying the Championship decal will not score points. Also, a letter indicating the class in which the car is entered should be displayed after the competition number. Competition numbers will be supplied at the beginning of the season.

AMERICAN/ENGLISH GLOSSARY OF AUTOMOTIVE TERMS

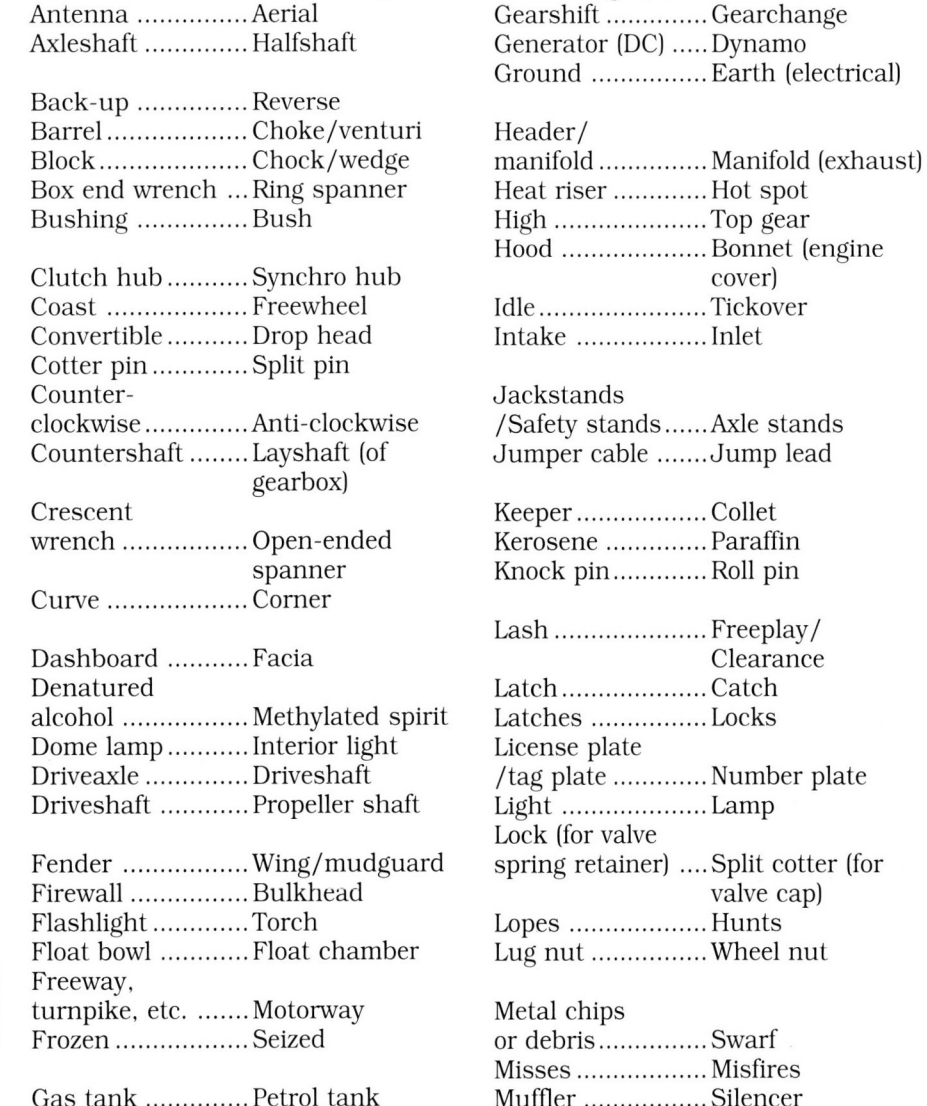

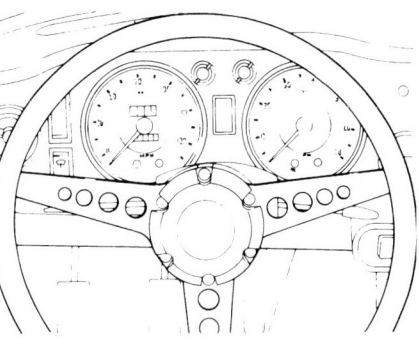

American	English	American	English
A-arm	Wishbone suspension)	Gas pedal	Accelerator pedal
Antenna	Aerial	Gasoline (gas)	Petrol
Axleshaft	Halfshaft	Gearshift	Gearchange
		Generator (DC)	Dynamo
Back-up	Reverse	Ground	Earth (electrical)
Barrel	Choke/venturi		
Block	Chock/wedge	Header/manifold	Manifold (exhaust)
Box end wrench	Ring spanner	Heat riser	Hot spot
Bushing	Bush	High	Top gear
		Hood	Bonnet (engine cover)
Clutch hub	Synchro hub	Idle	Tickover
Coast	Freewheel	Intake	Inlet
Convertible	Drop head		
Cotter pin	Split pin	Jackstands/Safety stands	Axle stands
Counter-clockwise	Anti-clockwise	Jumper cable	Jump lead
Countershaft	Layshaft (of gearbox)	Keeper	Collet
		Kerosene	Paraffin
Crescent wrench	Open-ended spanner	Knock pin	Roll pin
Curve	Corner	Lash	Freeplay/Clearance
		Latch	Catch
Dashboard	Facia	Latches	Locks
Denatured alcohol	Methylated spirit	License plate/tag plate	Number plate
Dome lamp	Interior light	Light	Lamp
Driveaxle	Driveshaft	Lock (for valve spring retainer)	Split cotter (for valve cap)
Driveshaft	Propeller shaft		
		Lopes	Hunts
Fender	Wing/mudguard	Lug nut	Wheel nut
Firewall	Bulkhead		
Flashlight	Torch	Metal chips or debris	Swarf
Float bowl	Float chamber	Misses	Misfires
Freeway, turnpike, etc.	Motorway	Muffler	Silencer
Frozen	Seized		
Gas tank	Petrol tank		

157

American	English	American	English	American	English
Oil pan	Sump	(of differential)	Crownwheel	Taper pin	Cotter pin
Open flame	Naked flame	Rocker panel	Sill panel	Teardown	Strip(down) dismantle
Panel wagon/van	Van	Rod bearing	Big-end bearing	Throw-out bearing	Thrust bearing
Parking light	Sidelight	Rotor/disk	Disc (brake)	Tie-rod	Trackrod (of steering)
Parking brake	Handbrake	Secondary shoe	Trailing shoe (of brake)	Transmission	Gearbox
Piston pin or wrist pin bearing	Small (little) end bearing	Sedan	Saloon	Troubleshooting	Fault finding/diagnosis
Piston pin or wrist pin	Gudgeon pin	Setscrew, Allen screw	Grub screw	Trunk	Boot
Pitman arm	Drop arm	Shift fork	Selector fork	Tube wrench	Box spanner
Power brake booster	Servo unit	Shift lever	Gearlever/gearstick	Turn signal	Indicator
Primary shoe	Leading shoe (of brake)	Shift rod	Selector rod	Valve lifter	Tappet
Prussian blue	Engineer's blue	Shock absorber, shock	Damper/shocker	Valve lifter or tappet	Cam follower or tappet
Pry	Prise (force apart)	Snap-ring	Circlip	Valve cover	Rocker cover
Prybar	Crowbar	Soft top	Hood	VOM (volt ohmmeter)	Multimeter
Prying	Levering	Spacer	Distance piece		
		Spare tire	Spare wheel	Wheel cover	Roadwheel trim
Quarter window	Quarterlight	Spark plug wires	HT leads	Wheel well	Wheelarch
		Spindle arm	Steering arm	Whole drive line	Transmission
Recap	Retread	Stablizer or sway bar	Anti-roll bar	Windshield	Windscreen
Release cylinder	Slave cylinder	Station wagon	Estate car	Wrench	Spanner
Repair shop	Garage	Stumbles	Hesitates		
Replacement	Renewal				
Ring gear		Tang or lock	Tab		

158

INDEX

AC 7, 9
Aeroquip hoses 85
Alfa Romeo 7, 40, 52
Alvis 9
Armstrong Siddeley 9
Aston Martin 9
Austin 9,11,19
Austin-Healey 3000 7, 54, 127
Australian Motor Manual 128, 129
Autocar 38-40, 42,127
Auto-Union 32

Bentley 9
Beaufighter 11
Belgrove, Walter 13, 14, 16, 17, 21
Birmingham 72
Black, John 10-17, 19
BMW 8, 12, 32, 52
bodyshells 72, 73, 85, 86
Bosch 79, 82
Bristol 9
British Cars 131
British Heritage 72, 73
British Leyland 42, 46, 50, 132
Brock, Pete 91
Browning guns 16
Buckles, Peter 72
Buick 8, 11

Callaby, Frank 13
Car and Driver 31, 40, 46, 92, 126, 127
Carrozzeria Touring 14
Cars & Car Conversions 129
Caterham Seven 130
Champion spark plugs 51, 89
chassis 58, 59, 63, 68-72
Citroen 9
Chevrolet 8, 40
Chrysler 11
Cobra Daytona 91
Coventry 11, 14, 16, 21, 43, 53, 54
Cox, Peter 72, 86
Cox & Buckles Championship 95-117
Cox & Buckles Spares 72
Custom Car 45, 130

Daimler 9
Datsun 240Z 43, 46, 94, 130
Datsun 260Z 94
Datsun 280Z 94
Datsun SRL311 2000 Roadster 93, 94

Day, Dennis 94
David Brown Tractors 9
De Havilland Aircraft Co. 17
De Tomaso Pantera 46
Dittemore, Jim 91, 93
Dodge 8, 11
Donald Healey Motor Co. 9
Duckhams 89
Dunlop 21, 35, 36
Durkopp 32

Earls Court Motor Show, 1950 13

Ferguson tractors 11, 17
Ferrari 8
Fiat 35, 40, 42, 52
Firestone tyres 93
Fitzgerald, Jim 94
Flowers, Neville and Raymond 21, 22
Ford 8, 9, 13, 32, 42, 54, 130
Frazer Nash 9
fuel injection 8, 28, 29 73, 75, 77-83, 87, 89, 119, 126-128, 131, 132

Giesecke, Gerhart 34, 35
Girling 21
Goodyear 36
Grinham, Ted 16, 17, 19, 21, 28
Group 44 91, 93, 94

Healey, Donald 16
Hercules engine 11
Hillman 9
H M Hobson (Aircraft & Motor Components) Ltd 12
Hopfinger, Bernard 32
Hot Car 129
HRG 9
Humber 9
Hurst/Airheart brake calipers 93
Hutton, Ray 128, 129

Idle 9
interior trim 62, 67, 127, 132
Invicta 9

Jaguar D-Type 21
Jaguar E-Type 8, 42, 46, 54
Jaguar Mk II 8
Jaguar XK120 9, 13
Jaguar XK150 87, 88

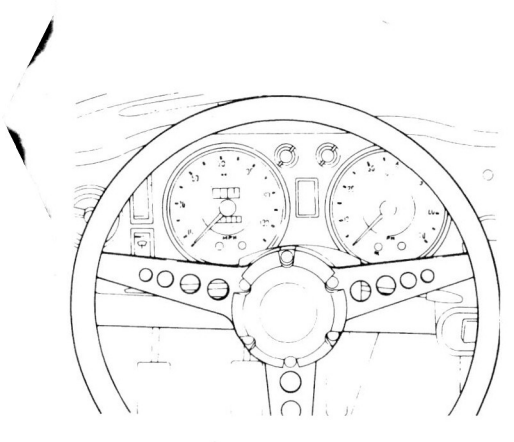

159

Jaguar XJR 93
Jensen 9
Jensen-Healey 87, 94, 130, 131
Johnson, Alan 93
Jowett 9

Kamm, Wunibald 35
Kangol safety belts 49
Karmann GmbH, Wilhelm 8, 32, 34, 36, 127, 132
Kastner, RW 'Kas' 91
King, Spen 88
Koenig-Fachsenfeld, Baron 34
Koni 93, 130

Lagonda 9
Laycock de Normanville gearbox 48, 49, 76, 132
Lea-Francis 9
Leyland Motors 26
Lloyd 9
Lord, Leonard 10
Lotus Elan 42, 46
Lotus Eleven 21
Lotus wheels 93
Lyons, William 11
Lucas 28, 52, 75, 78, 79, 81, 82, 87-89, 127, 132

McComb, John 91, 94
McWilliams, Bruce 29, 35, 43
Mansell, Nigel 94
Mazda RX-2 46
Meadows Frisky 21
MG 9, 52
MG Midget 72, 73, 86
MG RV8 54
MG TC 13
MG TD 15
MG TF 15
MGB 40, 72, 73, 86, 87, 130, 131
MGC 7, 42, 54
MGF 8, 54
Michelin 35, 36, 129, 130
Michelotti, Giovanni 8, 22, 25, 34, 131, 132
Millar, Alan 29
Minter, Milt 93
Morgan 9, 42, 87, 130, 131
Morris 9, 11, 131
Mosquito 11
Moss Europe 59, 72, 73, 79, 86
Motor 42, 127-129
Motor Racing & Sportscar 128, 129
Motor Sport 44, 48, 87, 89
Mueller, Lee 94

Newman, Paul 91, 94
Nuffield, Lord 10, 11
Nuffield Organisation 9

Opel GT 46
Oxford aeroplane 11

Paris Show, 1950 12
Peichl, Rolf 34
Peugeot 205GTI 54
Plymouth 8
Princess Margaret 13
Pininfarina 14
Pontiac 8, 35
Popular Imported Cars 126, 127
Porsche 32, 93, 94, 128
Pumfords 82

Racetorations 59, 72, 82, 86, 117, 125
Ray, Jim 94
Reliant Scimitar 42
Renault 4 99
Richardson, Clive 44, 48, 87-89
Richardson, Ken 18-20
Riley 9
Road & Track 31, 126, 129
Road Test 31, 38, 127-9
Rolls-Royce 9
Rootes Group 9, 11, 12
Rootes, William 10
Rossi, Steven 26
Rostyle wheel covers 36, 42, 132
Rover 12
Rubery Owen 72
rust 59-67, 70-72

Saab Sonnet 46
Sebring 91
shadow factories 11
Sharpe, Bob 93
Singer 9
Slough 9
Speke 41, 72
Sports Car World 38, 129, 130
SS Cars 11
Standard 8, 27
Standard 2.0-litre engine 18
Standard Flying Nine 15
Standard Motor Company 11-14, 17
Standard-Triumph 9, 13, 16, 19-21, 26
Standard Vanguard 13-15
SU carburettors 83

Sunbeam Alpine Tiger 7
Sunbeam-Talbot 9

Thames Ditton 9
Thomas Ward & Co. 12
Triumph 9, 11, 12, 16, 17, 89, 91
Triumph 20TS 14, 15, 19
Triumph 1800 Roadster 10, 12, 13
Triumph 2000 27
Triumph Mayflower 17, 18
Triumph Renown 17
Triumph Stag 43, 44, 48, 85
Triumph Town and Country saloon 13
Triumph TR2 19, 20, 131
Triumph TR3 21-23, 91
Triumph TR3A 23-25, 91
Triumph TR4 26-29, 34, 91, 127, 131
Triumph TR4A 28-31
Triumph TR5 28, 30-32, 34-36, 38, 50, 75, 88, 93, 126-128, 131, 132
Triumph TR7 50, 53, 54, 87, 91, 94, 95
Triumph TR8 91
Triumph TR250 29, 34-36, 91, 93, 127
Triumph TR 250K 91-93
Triumph TRX (Bullet) 12-14
Tullius, Bob 91, 93, 94
Turin 22
Turnbull, John 19
Tustin, Martin 21, 22
TVR Vixen S2 42

Uprichard, Darryl 59, 72, 86

Vauxhall 9
Vignale 22, 25, 26
Volkswagen Beetle 32
Volkswagen Golf GTI 54
Volkswagen Karmann-Ghia 32, 40, 46
Volvo 1800ES 46

Weber carburettors 83, 92, 119
Webster, Harry 16-19, 21, 26, 27, 34
What Car? 130, 131
Wheels 128
Wolseley 9

Yenko Corvair Stinger 94

Zenith Stromberg carburettors 29, 45, 46, 51, 83, 132

DEAR READER,
WE HOPE YOU ENJOYED THIS VELOCE PRODUCTION. IF YOU HAVE IDEAS FOR BOOKS ON TRIUMPH OR OTHER MARQUES, PLEASE WRITE AND TELL US.
MEANTIME, HAPPY MOTORING!

THE END